Collecting Antique Marbles

Collecting Antique Marbles

SECOND EDITION

Paul Baumann

WALLACE-HOMESTEAD BOOK COMPANY   Radnor, Pennsylvania

Copyright © 1970, 1991 by Paul Baumann

Second Edition   All Rights Reserved

Published in Radnor, Pennsylvania 19089, by Wallace-Homestead,
a division of Chilton Book Company

No part of this book may be reproduced, transmitted or stored
in any form or by any means, electronic or mechanical,
without prior written permission from the publisher

Designed by Adrianne Onderdonk Dudden
Manufactured in the United States of America

Library of Congress Cataloging in Publication Data
Baumann, Paul, 1946-
    Collecting antique marbles / Paul Baumann.—2nd ed.
      p.   cm.
    Includes index.
    ISBN 0-87069-569-X (pbk.)
    1. Marbles (Game)—Collectors and collecting.   I. Title.
NK6215.B32   1990
688.7′62—dc20   90-70540
                                         CIP

2 3 4 5 6 7 8 9 0 1   2 1 0 9 8 7 6 5 4 3

Front cover: German Swirls with Latticinio Cores.

Back cover: Lutz-Mica Rainbow Onionskin. One of only two known. Author's collection.

Color and black and white photographs by Mary Circelli and Barbara Vogel.

CONTENTS

ACKNOWLEDGMENTS

I am constantly amazed that I am writing a second edition to my book *Collecting Antique Marbles,* and that the first edition has sold well over a 20 year period. My first thank you should probably go to the original editorial staff of the Wallace-Homestead Book Company, who, in 1969, agreed to publish my book. Remember, at that time there were no national marble clubs (no marble clubs of any kind), no marble meets or shows, no marbles featured on TV or in *Smithsonian Magazine.* When asked (and I was) I could give no data on how many other marble collectors there might be. In spite of this Wallace-Homestead took a chance on my book, even paying for the photography. My second thank you would have to go to all the marble collectors and enthusiasts who purchased that book over the last 20 years. You are the folks who have made this second edition possible.

The two decades which have passed since the writing of the first edition have seen an explosion in marble information (at least in some areas) and in collector sophistication (in all areas). As interest, sophistication, and prices have risen, smaller and smaller variations in marbles have become important in determining value. Thus more subgroups will be discussed in this book. The existence of marble shows has also made it possible for collectors to routinely view marbles of such rarity that most collectors would never have seen one in 30 or even 50 years of pre-show collecting. Because of these factors, I needed much more help in writing the second edition than I did writing the first. I also needed to draw on other people's collections to have good representation of all the types discussed.

At the end of this book is a list crediting those collectors who lent marbles for the plates in this book. That list specifies which marbles were donated by plate, but I would like to acknowledge those collectors here as well; it takes a dose of steady nerves, generosity, and a lot of patience to lend someone hundreds or thousands of dollars' worth of breakable objects for an indefinite time period. Collectors with the fortitude to do this include Lorain Altshuler, Roland Baker,

Jamie Browder, Beverly Brule, Sue Cooper, Gary Dolly, Tom Ecker, Frank Gardenhire, Earl Hogue, Elizabeth Reeb, and Bucky Zelesky. Some collectors served double duty, supplying both marbles and information. Among these were Dick Davidson, who put me on the track of the Seip Mound marbles; Brian Estepp, who provided history of the Christensen Agate Co. at Cambridge, Ohio; Lloyd Huffer, who sent me copies of the rules for games played on the General Grant board; David Johnson, who did antiques shop marble surveys in two cities; Roger Matile, who shared his knowledge of French-Canadian voyagers; and Larry Prince, who not only provided the Roman marble photos but the information to accompany them.

The information on marbles in this book was built on the foundation of information supplied for my first edition. Among those whose information is still as useful today as it was 20 years ago are Mr. Earl Fosnaught, Mrs. Meta E. Gunderson, and Mr. M.G. (Fred) Wright.

Important new information has come from a variety of sources. Jeff Carskadden made his prolific research findings and top-flight collection of clay, crockery, and china marbles available to me, as well as supplying me with a photo of the tricolored horse sulphide. He also lent me his copy of Der Universal Spielwaren Katalog and early catalog information from Our Traveler, Butler Brothers, City Products, and Baltimore Bargain House. Bert Cohen provided me with lots of early marble articles and lots of friendship. Mike Cohill did as much marble research in the last six months as the rest of us have in the last 20 years. He then graciously shared the results of his enthusiasm and effort. Jim Davis got the scoop on Betty Boop and passed it along. Craig Gamache provided early catalog information from William Croft & Sons, Toronto. Steve Hartman provided information on sulphide marbles. The story on Lutz marbles in bank signs was provided by J.E. McGuire. The majority of my carpet bowl information from game rules to rarity was possible through the kind assistance of John Moore. The Stephan Pfnur family in Germany not only sent much information on the early stone marble industry, but sent a free marble as well. Art Ward provided insights into the rarity of sulphide marbles. Fred Weinrich gave me local history and early dates for some types of marbles. Several collectors supplied me with information on marbles in their collections including Laura Askerman, Frank Amrheim, Bud Braunlich, Mrs. W. A. Hall, Stan Okasaki, and Doris and Greg Stake.

A number of institutions and professionals also supplied me with information. History on the old German glass marbles was provided in part by Museum fur Glaskunst in Lauscha and the Deutches Spielzeugmuseum in Sonneberg, both in the province of Thuringen, Germany. I am also indebted to the Ohio Historical Society, particularly Martha Potter Otto in Columbus, Ohio and curator Jay Snyder of the Rutherford B. Hayes Presidential Home and Museum in Freemont, Ohio. (Also thanks to Gary Huxford, whose article on the latter museum in Marble Mart/Newsletter Issue 33 put me on the trail.) A big thanks to Bill Deal of the Navarre-Bethlehem Township Historical Society for his educational winter tour. Also thanks to Dr. Mike Chipperfield of the Ohio State University Art Department for information on the methods used in the production of china and pottery spheres. Another professional is glass artist Mark Mathews who was kind enough to invite us into his studio and allow us to photograph some of his techniques. Don Taylor's help was invaluable in forming the price guide. I also owe a debt of gratitude to Nancy Demarchi, whose computer skills and dedication to this project enabled this book to be completed in a timely manner.

Finally I need to acknowledge the contribution of my family. My mother Helene and father Chris (81 and 83 at the time I write this) gave me my love of antiques and collecting, and humored my desire to research and write a marble book rather than get a paying job when I came home from my first year of college in 1965. When I was just a small boy, my father gave me a portion of his marble collection and taught me what to look for in the antiques shops. Many of the marbles pictured in this book were collected by my father who started acquiring them in the 1930s. My wife Denise and son Brendan have encouraged me all the way and have sacrificed a great deal of time with me. They have put up with unshoveled walks in winter, long grass in summer, and lonely days and nights as I've fed untold hours into this book. We are all looking forward to catching up on family activities, and I thank them for their great patience.

Paul C. Baumann
July, 1990

Collecting Antique Marbles

INTRODUCTION

Welcome to the joy and excitement of collecting marbles. Antique marbles bring forth emotions matched by few other collectible items. Most antiques are collected for rarity, beauty, or craftsmanship. Certainly, antique marbles have these qualities. The early ones were made by individual craftsmen whose skills are only now being rediscovered by a few modern artists. These early craftsmen substituted skill and patience for technology, making small works of art that continue to appreciate in value. The wide range of variation in style and color, a hallmark of handmade items, make marbles an exciting collectible. Their beauty makes them a wonderful display item. Their size makes them easy to display.

Two other things really set marble collecting off from the collecting of most other antiques—a sense of history and childhood memories. Many of us played marbles in our youth or had friends who did. Children still play marbles today; in fact the game is becoming popular again. Companionship, healthy competition, the joy of winning, the agony of defeat, a less complicated time; all of these memories are evoked when we view marbles. These sorts of emotions set marble collectors apart from collectors of things like art glass or oil paintings. The collections of many marble addicts are not grounded in beauty alone, or in the intrinsic value or possibility of appreciation of the items in their collection. Instead they are grounded in a fondness for remembering and reliving some of their childhood fun and freedom.

Marble collectors also have a very strong sense of history; not only their own history of playing marbles and later collecting marbles, but the history of those who went before them: their father, their grandfather, their great-grandfather—and let's not forget grandmother and great-grandmother; not all sharpshooters were boys! We can go much farther back in history than just our great-grandparents. Marbles are one of the few toys that have been played with for centuries or even for millennia. How many other sports, games, or toys (and marbles are all three) could make such a statement? Baseball, football and basketball are all products of the last century or so. Toy trains and trucks go back only a few decades, and even teddy bears have their origin with President Roosevelt in the first decade of the 1900s. In fact, how many games can you think of that a child living today, a child living during the Civil War, and a child living during the Revolutionary War would all know and understand? Marbles probably go much further back than that to prehistoric times. While things like cameo glass are only a dot in the long history of mankind, marbles represent a line running through history, beginning with the dawn of civilization and continuing until today. It is this line that connects those of us today who collect marbles with all the generations of children who have come before us, marching back through the centuries. I know, at least for myself, it is this aspect of marbles which gives me a sense of oneness with all those other children who knelt down with their companions to play a game of skill and to build friendships. I think this may be the reason that marble shows or marble meets seem more like a gathering of old and new friends than a gathering of investors with various degrees of expertise.

My own marble collection was the direct result of my parents being very avid antiques collectors. Therefore, as a young boy I discovered that I was going to spend a lot of time in antiques shops whether I enjoyed it or not. Since this was the case, I decided I might as well enjoy it and start collecting something. What caught my eye were the old marbles. Being a marble player at school, I was naturally attracted to the antique ones, of which my father already had a nice collection. My father, realizing that it would enhance his chances for peace and quiet if I was happy also, gave me part of his collection (the swirl and crockery marbles), helped me learn how to identify the old ones, and advised me on what to purchase in the shops. Since that time I have been a confirmed marble collector and have never regretted the choice I made in my early years.

Where should you go to collect antique marbles? Of course the most common hunting ground is the antiques shop, antiques show, flea market, or auction. Different parts of the country vary in the numbers and types of old marbles found. To give you an idea of what to expect in parts of the Midwest, a friend and I surveyed 88 antiques shops in Columbus, Ohio and Springfield, Illinois. Of these 28% were specialty shops with no marbles, and another 38% didn't deal in marbles or have much interest. This left 23% which occasionally had marbles (but not at the time), and 11% which actually had some in the shop to sell. Your best bet to fight these odds is to build a relationship with specific dealers so they'll call you first when they get a new batch of marbles.

A good idea for a new collector is to visit a collector in the area who has had the hobby for a few years, or an antiques dealer who has had some experience with marbles. Most collectors are very friendly and will gladly share some of their time to show a beginning collector what the different types of old marbles look like, and to give some hints on what and where to start collecting. When I was a boy I received free advice by the ton and even free marbles occasionally. However, marbles have shot up in price since then, and I can't guarantee the same results for anyone starting out today.

I highly recommend that new collectors specialize in a particular area. Look for a particular type of marble or one or two sub-groups that appeal to you. This will allow you to familiarize yourself more quickly with what is rare and what is common, and with the prices of the different types. On the other hand, it is nice to have a representative of all the different varieties in your collection. Besides, if you learn the basics of pricing in all the groups, you will be able to pick up a bargain in any type of marble, and then trade that one for the variety you collect.

Eventually, familiarization with your selected types of marbles will give you insight into differences in color and style which are not yet common knowledge. Thus you may be able to buy marbles that are currently undervalued and which will appreciate in the future. Groups of marbles with variety are best suited for these sorts of collections. For instance, onionskins have plenty of individual variations. Sulphides with figures of people could be collected, since there is so much variety available in the types of human figures and the things that the people in the marbles are doing or holding. At a lower price level, collecting sulphide dogs would be a good idea. Again there is variety among different breeds of dogs, positions of dogs, collars on dogs, bases that the dogs are on, or other factors. Also all the possible sub-groupings of sulphide dogs have not yet been listed in price guides, meaning that some of them are probably undervalued. This of course is just an example of the type of collection that could be made. The nice thing about marbles is that such collections are possible at almost any price range; all it takes is a little investigation.

Another good idea is to join one or more of the national marble societies that now exist. When my first book was published (*Collecting Antique Marbles*, Wallace-Homestead Book Company, 1970), no organization of marble collectors existed. The first of these, The Marble Collectors Society of America, was founded in 1976 by Stan Block. Two other national societies, Marble Collectors Unlimited and The National Marble Club of America, have come into existence. Several regional clubs have also started up and some of them are expanding rapidly. Names and addresses for the three national organizations can be found in the appendix at the back of the book. Each of the national societies puts out a newsletter which gives information on collecting and provides a forum for people who want to buy or sell marbles. The subscription to one or more of these newsletters is a sure way for a beginning collector to start to learn the ins and outs of marble mania. The buy and sell sections of these publications can also provide a better idea of current pricing than price guides or books which are revised only once every several years. These organizations also sponsor the marble meets or get-togethers that were mentioned previously. Such meets are great places to mix with other collectors and learn about the hobby, not to mention being great places to pick up that unusual marble which might take years to locate in an antiques shop.

Of course for those with an archaeological or treasure hunting bent, you can always dig for marbles rather than purchase them. This type of collecting is difficult however, and it's best if one first locates a spot where marbles are likely to be found. Sites occupied by early glass factories which may have made marbles is one such location. Digging around such areas will sometimes turn up specimens. Also the grounds around old school buildings, old homes, or old park areas can sometimes be productive. Marbles have been found in archaeological excavations of both cisterns and privies. However, don't attempt hunting marbles this way unless you know beforehand that some have been found in the area you intend to work, or unless you have spare time and don't mind spending some of it with little possibility of finding much of any real value. Of course when you do find something you have the advantage of knowing the area in which it was used or produced. Perhaps you can even date your find by dating other items found near it. Published accounts of marbles found at archaeological sites will be mentioned in the upcoming chapters.

A Brief History of Marbles

As mentioned previously, marbles have an extremely old origin and represent one of the earliest games ever played. A number of articles, beginning back in the 1860s (Patten, 1869) assert that marbles were played with by Egyptian, Greek, or Roman children and at least one of these articles (*The Mentor*, 1927) states that marbles used by Egyptian and Roman children are contained in the British Museum. Larry Prince, a New York collector, had some German friends checking the antiques stores in that country in the hopes of finding some of the early glass marbles produced in Germany. Instead of antiques what he got were antiquities—two ancient marbles (pictured in Plate 28A). Larry had these marbles evaluated by antiquities expert Kenneth Linsner. His report stated that the marble with the spots of color, more accurately the indigo and millefiore glass sphere, was "probably" from Egypt and "certainly" dated from the Roman period about the second century A.D. Linsner reports that he found both a fissure in the glass and an attempt at drilling. He conjectures that the drilling may have ceased when the fissure was discovered, since it would have split the glass had the drilling continued. Thus he feels this sphere was probably intended as a bead from the outset and that such beads were commonly used in necklaces during that time.

However, such was not the case with the second sphere, described as being of green glass with a high iron content and iridescent weathering overall. Linsner stated that this marble was undoubtedly Roman in origin. Similar high iron glasses first became abundant in the first century B.C., and Linsner felt it would be "plausible" to date this sphere to the first or second century A.D. Linsner further stated that Athenaeus, a Roman writer of the late first century A.D., included in his *Panegyricus in Pisonem* a reference to the game of marbles. In his story the suitors of Penelope in the Odyssey shot their "alleys" against another marble representing the queen. The first one to hit the queen marble had another turn, and if he were successful again he was considered to be the presumptive bridegroom. Linsner states that this episode is not recorded in the Homeric Epic itself, but if true would place the origins of the game of marbles well into the 9th century B.C. in Greece. He then wrote, "We can certainly state that the game was actively played by the time of Athenaeus (180–200 A.D.) from his accurate description. That your sphere is an ancient Roman marble may be possible. There is very little else that it could be. Certainly glass spheroids were made for jewelry, but yours is $\frac{3}{4}''$ in diameter and is an unlikely candidate. It shows no attempt at drilling. I have yet to see other examples of this nature in my career, which includes three seasons of excavating the Hellenistic and Roman city of Aphrodisias in Caria. It may be that in our ignorance we have yet to separate out and question the nature of such spheroids as they relate to the 'Ludi' or informal games of the Romans."

Mark Randall (1971) states that the use of marbles is pre-Columbian in the New World. Clay spheres, according to Randall, were found in prehistoric southwestern United States pueblo ruins, in Classic period Valley of Mexico ruins, and in the northern plains. The Ohio Historical Society has on display in Columbus a series of stone spheres with incised designs on their surface which were taken from Indian mounds of the Hopewell culture dating to around 200 to 300 A.D. These five spheres were taken from the Seip mound excavations and were made of steatite or soap stone, a soft stone which had to be imported from the southern Appalachian Mountains. Large pipes carved in effigies of birds and dogs were also made from steatite by societies in Alabama and Tennessee and traded north to the Hopewell people of Ohio.

Martha Potter Otto, curator of the Ohio Historical Society, points out in a letter to Richard Davidson, an Ohio collector who inquired about the marbles, that it is impossible to know whether the spheres were used in a game. She states that during historic times American Indians in this area did not have any diversions comparable to our shooting marbles, and that the spheres may have been used for something completely different. However, in the original article on the excavation (Shetrone and Greenman, 1931) the point is made that the spheres were found in the burnt offering, adjacent to burial 13, which was the cremation of a child on a poorly constructed platform. "This coincidence suggests that these engraved spheres were used as marbles and that they had been intended for the remains of the child." Certainly it is both logical and appealing to believe that the game of marbles might have been devised at a very early period in a number of different cultures, when children would have first used naturally rounded stones in some sort of game, and then later would have progressed to carved stones or marbles made of clay.

We know for certain that marbles were played by children in Europe starting in the late Middle Ages. A manuscript from the 1400s (*Collectors Roundup*, 1947) refers to them as "the little balls with which school boys played and which are very cheap." The town council of Nuremberg in 1503 limited the playing of marble games to a meadow outside the town limits (Ferretti, 1974). The town council statutes in the English village of St. Gall authorized the sacristan of St. Laurence to use a cat-of-ninetails on boys "who played at marbles under the fish stand and refused to be warned off." In 1560 Pieter Breughel the Elder depicted children playing marbles as one of about eighty children's games illustrated in his painting entitled "Children's Games." English author Joseph Addison, in one of the articles he wrote for the early Dublin newspaper *"The Tatler"* in 1709 and 1710 referred to "a game of marbles not unlike our common taw." Daniel Defoe, author of *Robinson Crusoe*, wrote in 1720: "Marbles, which used to call children playing at bowls, yielded him a mighty diversion, and he was so dexterous an artist at shooting that little alabaster globe from between the end of his forefinger and knuckle of his thumb that he seldom missed hitting plumb, as the boys called it, the marble aimed at, though at a distance of two or three yards."

Some of the American presidents may also have been marble players. Three articles mention Washington, Jefferson, and Adams as having been marble collectors and/or players. Whether or not this information is correct is anybody's guess. Fred Ferretti (1974) goes further by saying that Abraham Lincoln was a sharpey at shooting marbles. He says Lincoln became "a marbles-playing terror," and his specialty was "old bowler." However, I haven't independently verified that Lincoln was a marble fanatic. The Hayes Presidential Center, a museum for President Rutherford B. Hayes at Fremont, Ohio, has a 2" + red onionskin marble in its collection. Hayes was married in 1852 and had eight children. While it is possible that the marble belonged to one of his children, it might also be part of an unrelated "local collection" donated to the museum at a later date. Sulphide marbles were apparently also made as campaign items for at least a couple of the American presidents. Presidents James Garfield (1881) and Benjamin Harrison (1889–1893) were pictured in sulphide marbles showing both their face and the face of their running mate. There are also marbles representing Teddy Roosevelt and William McKinley.

If presidents or their children did play with marbles, then what kinds of games did they play? Outdoor marble games, old and new, break down into basically three types. Circle games where marbles are shot out of a circle or some other small area with a boundary, chase games where two players alternately shoot at each other's marble, and hole games or target games where marbles are shot into an opening of some sort. Going through all the common names for marbles from different countries and different time periods and listing all the rules for all the different variations of marble games could take up most of this book. In fact, a couple of books have specialized in the area of marble games (Ferretti, 1973 and Runyan, 1985). I have limited my discussion of marble games to Chapter 8 where I describe some of the better known and more interesting diversions using marbles.

What's in a Name?

In my first edition I gave in to my instincts as a research biologist and developed a key for identifying glass marbles. It was the sort of key used by taxonomists to key out different kinds of animal and plant species. Core types and outer coloration were all assigned different numbers. Different combinations of numbers indicated different types of marbles. Unfortunately there were several major problems with this method. For one thing combinations of numbers were not very appealing to collectors. For instance, the term mica is easier to remember than 5-14-MC and the term Lutz is more romantic than 2-7G. The upshot of the lack of pizzazz and the complexity was that nobody bothered to use the system. In retrospect I can see that the system was too complex and too boring for the exciting subject of antique marbles. However, the system was precise, and by going to common names, which I'll do in this book, certain problems arise.

Common names, unfortunately, often mean different things to different people. Therefore they have to be defined carefully. Also one has to determine what characters to use to sub-divide groups of marbles. For instance, if goldstone is used merely as another addition to basic types of marbles such as spirals or swirls or onionskins, it becomes much less important than if goldstone marbles are singled out as a group. Similarly, are clambroths any marbles of white opaque glass, or are they any opaque marbles which have narrow, evenly spaced outer lines? Or are they marbles with both features (white with narrow, evenly spaced outer lines)? Such distinctions are important because they affect both the perceived rarity of the marble and its price. Above all one has to be consistent. You can't define clambroths as marbles of white opaque glass, and then turn around and call a black opaque marble a clambroth if it has evenly spaced lines as outer decoration.

I will divide marbles into chapters according to the materials from which they were made, how they were made, and who made them. For instance, stone marbles will constitute a chapter, clay, crockery and china another chapter, glass marbles another chapter, etc. Each of these chapters will further be divided, i.e. into types of stone, clay, glass, and so on. Glass marbles will be discussed by the core types since I believe that to be more important than outer decoration. Various core types include latticinio or net, solid, divided, ribbon, opaque, and onionskins. Peppermints, flags, and mica will also be discussed in this chapter. Carpet bowls, though made from a crockery material, will be discussed in a separate chapter in order to give an in-depth look into the history and rules of the game(s).

The history and techniques of producing cane cut marbles will be discussed in a separate chapter as will individually-made marbles and transition and machine-made marbles. The chapter on individually made marbles will include end-of-day, cloud and paperweight, and sulphides. Transition and machine-made marbles will include a discussion of each and their manufacturers. A chapter on the various types of games using marbles is also included.

Valuation and Pricing

Theoretically, placing a value on marbles should be simple. By determining the marble's rarity and then looking at its size and condition one should be able to come up with a price. But what is rarity? It depends on how you lump or split categories of marbles. For instance, dogs are a real common figure in sulphide marbles. But how about dogs sitting up and begging? Are latticinio core swirls common? Yes. Are marbles with red latticinio cores common? No. The sophistication of marble collectors has grown as their opportunity to meet and exchange information has increased, and as information published about marbles has become more available. As the sophistication of collectors has increased, smaller and smaller variations in style and color have become important in the valuation of a marble. However, some choices have to be made on how far to sub-divide things. For instance, if we categorize dogs by position (standing, sitting, sitting up and begging, etc.) should we then categorize them further by species or appearance? Should we have a category for dogs with curly tails who are sitting up and begging? Or a category for dogs with curly tails with collars that are sitting up and begging? Some of these finer sub-divisions will have to wait for the next revision, probably in another twenty years. There just isn't enough information right now to accurately determine relative rarity of some of these sub-groups. For instance, I know that both camels with one hump and camels with two humps were produced in sulphides. But I have no real firm grasp on which of the two, if either, is any rarer. Therefore camels will just be listed as one group in the price guide.

It is in areas like this where collectors still have a chance to beat the market. If a collector specializes in a particular area and knows more than the current books on the subject, he can then purchase marbles which are currently undervalued and which will appreciate more than marbles whose rarity is already known. In fact, the sharp collector will read this book not only to find out what new sub-groups have been recognized but also to find out what sub-groups he or she knows about that have not yet been recognized. For instance, this book contains new information on patterns in china marbles and carpet bowls. However, there is no information given on different colors used on those marbles and bowls nor what their relative rarity might be. Collectors who specialize in these can then get some information which is not held by the general collecting public.

Having more or less disposed of rarity, we now proceed to size. One would think that size would be an easy thing to factor into pricing. But large size is worth more for some types of marbles than for others. For instance, size is quite important in determining the value for a swirl. However, size is not as important in determining the value of a sulphide when the rarity of the figure is of overriding importance. Sometimes you will see two sulphides in which the size of the figure is identical, but one marble will have more glass and be larger. You might also see two sulphides where the size of the marble is the same, but one figure is larger than the other. So which size is important in determining the value; the size of the figure or the size of the marble? In my personal opinion size is so unimportant in the value of sulphides that I'm not even going to present prices for different size groups. However I suspect in reality collectors will still pay a premium for larger marbles with larger figures. Also bigger is not always better. The vast majority of swirl marbles were produced for playing and were about $\frac{5}{8}''$ to $\frac{3}{4}''$ in diameter. Marbles smaller than this size group as well as those larger than this size group were produced in much fewer numbers, and therefore are much rarer.

Even condition varies somewhat in its influence on price depending upon the value of the marble involved. A large chip on a $\frac{5}{8}''$ brown Bennington is probably cause for depositing it in the trash can. However the same can't be said of a large chip on a colored glass sulphide. If you feel like putting it in a trash can please call me first and let me know, I'll be happy to take it off your hands. Of course, poor condition always reduces the value of a marble. But the reduction in value is directly dependent upon the rarity of the marble. In order to make things easy on myself, all of the prices in the guide will be based on marbles in mint condition.

Now that we've taken all three—rarity, size, and condition—into account we should be ready to price our marbles. Well, not quite. There is another elusive factor, perhaps best called pizzazz, which figures into the price of a marble. The prime example of this is the Lutz. The sparkling goldstone used in the Lutz marbles has caught the eye and captured the imagination of collectors. All of us, I think, would readily pay more money for something that is attractive than for another item which might be equally rare but comparatively dull. The only way to measure pizzazz is to look at prices being paid in the marketplace for different types of marbles. Prices in this book will reflect values being paid for marbles in the Midwest at this particular time. Such values may vary among different sections of the country.

There is also a final problem, namely how to price marbles that are extremely rare and seldom sold, or how to price marbles that are a new sub-group recently split off from other more common marbles that look similar. For instance Chapter 2 details a new distinctive group of crockery marbles which are superficially very similar to Benningtons. How could a price be established for these, since in most instances they've been sold for the same price as a normal Bennington? Also there are certain sub-groups which are routinely sold and for which prices are established, but which are undervalued in the current market. Here is where I'm going to go out on a limb. In the price guide for these sub-groups I'm not only giving the current price, which is based on retail value today, but I'm going to put an asterisk indicating that the marble is undervalued when its relative rarity is compared to that of other groups. Admittedly this is sort of like a stockbroker giving a buy signal. Like the stockbroker and his client, it's going to be your money, not mine, that is at risk, and I don't give any iron clad guarantees that the value of these marbles will increase. One final thought about using price guides. The absolute value of a marble can be out of date quickly. However, if you use relative rarity or relative prices, the price guide can be useful for years and years, even long after the original values are out of date. Good luck in finding those bargains!

◦1◦
Stone, Agate, and Semiprecious Stones

Stone

The very first marbles ever played with were probably stone. They were not made of stone but were stones; rounded stones found by children in stream beds and used in simple games. Since then stone has been used for making marbles, beginning with citizens of prehistoric cultures and ranging down through the ages, well into the 1900s. However few collectors will ever encounter any of the stone spheres from prehistoric cultures or even any of the alabaster or marble spheres used in England in the 15th and 16th centuries. Instead, I will begin by describing the small stone spheres which were first produced in great numbers in Germany with the help of water mills.

These marble mills are first mentioned in old manuscripts which date back to the beginning of the 17th century and which come from the Salzburg and Berchtesgaden regions of Germany. Already by 1680 this stone marble trade and marble milling was registered for tax purposes by the Prince-Bishop's court in Salzburg. One marble mill near Untersberg was founded in 1683 on the banks of a mountain stream called the Almbach. This mill, now owned by Pfnur family, has been in continuous operation for over 300 years, making it one of the oldest businesses in Bavaria. (The Pfnur family graciously answered my inquiry and supplied much of the information being presented here.) During the late 1600s and early 1700s, most of the production was from small family owned mills located on equally small mountain streams in the alps. These mills were run by mountain farmers and their families who had difficulty supporting themselves by agriculture and forestry alone. Not until the late 18th and 19th centuries did larger mills come into existence that produced great quantities of marbles. Concentrations of these larger mills were built both in Saxony and in Thuringen, a province in what was East Germany. The Saxony area includes the city of Coburg in western Germany.

In the Berchtesgaden region the marble milling industry peaked between 1780 and 1790. Back then the Almbach provided power for about 40 mills. Three other rivers in the area supported about 30 mills apiece. This expansion in the industry was caused by a boom in exports in the 1780s. The main customers were Northern Germany, England, and Holland. Although the marble balls were exported primarily as toys, they were used for many other purposes as well. Sailing ships liked to use them as ballast. The balls had one great advantage over sand; at the end of the trip they could be sold. In this manner, marbles from Berchtesgaden went all the way to the East and West Indies. During the 1780s up to 1,000 "hundredweights" (a hundredweight was approximately 10,000 marbles) were exported annually. By 1800 there were still approximately 600 mills in the Berchtesgaden region, especially on Salzburg's sovereign territory. However the average annual production already declined to approximately 300 hundred-weights. Merchants from Salzburg bought up the majority of this, in order to ship it to Nuremberg, Frankfurt, Cologne, Amsterdam and even farther north.

There are two articles which describe the marble cutting and milling industry in different areas of Germany in the last half of the 1800s. The first of these was obtained through my correspondence with the Deutsches Spielzeugmuseum (German Toy Museum) at Sonneberg, Thuringen. It is a copy of an article from an old book or magazine describing the production of these old stone marbles in the Sonneberg area. The description of this production in the following paragraphs is from a translation of this article, which itself was compiled in 1927 from a hand written study by a Mr. Friedel, a teacher in Megersgereuth. Interestingly the German Toy Museum has in its collection an original old mill from the same Almbach River where the last of the old marble mills is still in operation. The museum describes this mill as a dwarf compared to the Thuringen mills, both because it is from an earlier period, and because it was situated in the Alpine brooks where there is very little room to put a mill.

Two groups of people were needed to produce the stone marbles: the marble cutters and the marble millers. Let us accompany the former on his way to work in the Trudenthal region. In the early morning he left his shabby dwelling and went to his "Staloch" (small mine shaft) that he had set up in the area of the lower Muschelkalk. Muschelkalk, literally "mussel chalk," refers to a limestone formation with fossilized shells. Even relatively small mine shafts required long hard days of hand digging to reach the most productive layer. The cutter's clothing showed mending in spots, and a broad cap covered his head. Arrived at his place of work, he set up one or two ladders going to the depths. He usually worked lying down, on a horizontal passage that he had pushed into the layered stone. Only certain even layers of limestone, the so called "anchoring sediment," were sought after. When he had carefully detached enough plates from the hanging stones, he brought them through the tunnel to the mine shaft and carried them in baskets, usually on his head, into the open air. All of the family members helped in this task.

All of the stones went into a wooden cottage built near the mine. Benches were arranged along the walls. In front of the benches lay heavy plates of stone on wooden blocks. Now young and old grabbed the short handled hammers, sat down on the benches, and began to hammer the stone plates, still damp from the quarry, first into large stone cubes and then into smaller and smaller ones. Workers had to be industrious, because the marble miller was not noted for his good pay. When, after several days, many thousands of one size were on hand, the cubes were counted and brought in baskets or small wheelbarrows to the marble mill. The marble mill was usually an unassuming building, but it was located quite idyllically on a river. Rushing water drove the mill wheel. Creaking and grinding and clattering came out of the little house. The miner entered the moist, dim interior with caution. Several grinding procedures were in progress. He recognized the sturdy frames, each holding two millstone-like and identically sized plates. The lower plate was made of cast-iron and turned, while the upper plate of beechwood stood fixed in the so-called crib. Water ran constantly through the opening in the middle between the two plates to prevent unnecessary warming and to wash away the sludge being produced.

The miller stopped the driven wheel. While the wheel stood still, he winched upward the heavy beechwood plate. Both the upper surface of the iron plate and the underside of the covering plate had concentric grooves in which the small stone balls were rounded. He took out all of the balls and brought them to a collection box. He then put a new supply of stone cubes on the plate, taking them from the marble cutter who had just brought them in. The miller put fine sand over the cubes, let down the heavy beech plate and set the wheel in motion again. Grinding and banging, the stones began to move, and after six or eight hours the rounding process would be completed. Then the marble miller sorted the selected marbles, put them in the polishing barrel, poured on them a colored staining fluid, and added flowers of sulphur. Next he turned on the polishing barrel and let it revolve for hours, after which he could take from it the finished and shining marbles.

This marble industry had been practiced in the Sonneberg area probably since the Thirty Years War. It reached its first heyday around 1740 when a small group of immigrants from Salzberg came and perfected the technique of marble production. The second time of peak production was the period after the mid-19th century when German exporting rose appreciably. At that time one mine after another was opened especially in the area of Mengersgereuth, and marble mill upon marble mill was erected; twenty in the Effelden valley alone. But when in the 1870s the toy industry burgeoned, most of the marble miners of Thuringen turned to this healthier industry and the mines became ruins.

When that happened, the marble millers had to get their supply of cubes from the limestone areas of Sachsendorf and Veilsdorf or the regions of Spittelstein and Blumenrod near Coburg. When, in addition, competition rose from glass, porcelain, and clay marbles, the business of marble milling was no longer profitable, and one marble mill after another was abandoned. Only dammed-off brooks, ruins of mill wheels, and the remains of foundations remind us of the once great grinding mills.

Another article from a German newspaper recalls the experiences remembered by one of the last remaining marble cutters in Germany, Hermann Niller. At the time the article was written (1965) Mr. Miller had been traveling with his marble cutting tools to museums and exhibitions where he demonstrated the old art.

Mr. Niller was born in 1899 and lived in the town of Spittelstein, near Coburg. This is one of the towns from which the Thuringen mills had to buy their stones after the 1870s. At the turn of the century, the 80 to 100 marble cutters in the vicinity of Coburg were kept quite busy. Later, after the introduction of the clay marble industry, however, most of them, including Mr. Niller, became stone masons. At the age of 16 (1915) Mr. Niller took over his father's business. Quarries from which the marble was taken were usually at a depth of little more than 3 yards. Most of these quarries were situated in open fields. After the marble had been removed, the fields were smoothed over again and once more used for farm work. The limestone in the area was very good for making marbles, since it was easy to cut, and there was very little waste from crumbling in the grinding process.

On dry days the marble cutters went to the quarry. A few owned their own quarries but in most cases they were leased from the owner for a small fee. Often enormous amounts of huge rocks had to moved out of the way to reach the rock strata suitable for marbles. Layers useful as building stones or as cobblestones were taken out and carefully piled in stacks. The marble stone was broken into large blocks by sledge hammers and transported into a barn or cottage which had been built next to the quarry. Large supplies had to be stored for use as material during the rainy season and winter months. Placing the stone in barns protected it from frost. Even a light frost would separate the fine layers of stone from one another, causing it to crack and splinter when the actual cutting began. Each of the large original blocks was 40 to 50 cm square (approximately 16″ to 20″) and weighed about 100 pounds. When these large blocks had been cut to brick size they were carried to the stone cutter's hut. Here they were placed beside a large anvil situated near a window. A huge stone served as the base for the anvil, and another smaller stone or wooden stool was the stone cutter's seat. The hammer used for cutting the marble was of strong steel and had a sharp end on one side and a dull blade on the other. With the dull blade the stone was split once or twice in the palm of the hand to create smaller plates. Next one of these plates was held against the edge of the anvil in such a way that a well-aimed blow from the sharp side of the hammer would split the stone into $1\frac{1}{2}$ cm (about $\frac{3}{5}$″) square fragments. These were then counted and packed by the thousand.

There was very little pay for this type of work. On the average a worker could cut between 40,000 and 50,000 stones per week for which he received only 12 to 15 marks ($3 to $4). Of course, there are experts in every field and marble cutting is no exception. Andreas Stubenrauch writes that an old master once told him of a competition in France where he cut 50,000 in 40 hours and only took second place. The price paid for the stone cubes by the mill was equally small. Mr. Niller remembers getting from 50 to 60 pfennig per thousand or approximately 15 cents. Fifty percent of this amount went out in wages, and in addition there were transportation costs, electricity and insurance. "Life was hard, but one was attached to one's profession." In the mills the stone cubes were shaped into balls. A water wheel drove an iron plate attached to a shaft. The iron plate, depending on its size, had 13 to 16 concentrically arranged grooves. A series of beechwood blocks held together by iron rings faced the grinding plate. A box of about 700 stones would be placed on top of the iron plate. As the water caused the plate to rotate, the stones moved around, grinding and rubbing against each other. After 30 to 45 minutes this grinding would have removed all the corners and edges, and the marble miller could tell from the sound that the process was completed. The marbles were then collected, washed and put into the marble box. During the milling process, the grooves in beechwood became deeper and deeper so that the edges of the blocks had to be taken down from time to time.

Barrels were used to polish the marbles. The barrel had the shape of an ordinary barrel but was lined with felt. In the middle of the barrel's side was a door which could be closed tightly, through which the barrel was filled and emptied. Both ends of the barrel were connected to an axle which rotated it and caused the stones inside to turn over and over, rubbing against one another. This constant friction caused the marbles to become very hot and burn the sulphur and coloring which had been added to them. When the marbles were removed from the polishing barrel they had become permanently red, blue, green, yellow, or black. A counting board which accommodated 5,000 marbles was used to fill specific orders for shipping.

Today, only museum pieces remain of the once flourishing trade in stone marbles, except for the marble mill on the Almbach owned by the Pfnur family. The little house by the mill has been converted into an inn and restaurant, but the mill still turns and marbles are still made as souvenirs for the guests and for sale to other tourists. In fact, there are seldom enough marbles on hand even for their guests, since the initial milling process takes 4 to 8 days and there is only enough room in the mill for 6 to 8 balls. After that the balls are sorted into finer and finer mills with smaller and smaller grooves three times, and the final polishing may take place at a lathe or wheel. Thus the production over a year is very limited. The balls made today are produced from Untersberg Marble (Plate 1, lower right corner). Thus it is interesting that marbles from different parts of Germany may have had different types of stone as the base, and some of the color variations seen in uncolored stones (Plate 1 center right) may represent stones from different regions of Germany. Hopefully further research will identify the areas and time periods when these different types of marbles were produced.

Most of the early stone marbles are small in size, ranging from $\frac{1}{2}''$ to $1\frac{1}{8}''$ in diameter. These were commonly sold in large lots to department stores. The Spring 1903 Sears and Roebuck, Co. catalog carried the following description of these marbles: "Marbles—common stone marbles" or "Mibbs," "Imported, unbreakable" not "cheap, domestic kinds." Sears sold them in bags of 1,000 weighing approximately 10 pounds each. You could buy either unpolished marbles at 50 cents a bag or "brightly polished" marbles for 60 cents a bag. The word polished here seems really to have meant colored. Collections of these marbles often include both colored (Plate 1, top and top right) and uncolored stones, although some of these marbles have been played with so much that it is difficult to tell whether they were originally colored or not. Brightly colored marbles are relatively scarce and come in the range of colors previously mentioned. Most, however, are fairly dull, varying from yellow or olive to a brownish, bluish or gray shade. If later research can establish a link between certain types of stone and periods or regions of production in Germany, these marbles should appreciate in value.

Sometimes it is hard to distinguish between these stone marbles and china or clay marbles which were in poor condition. One difference is that these marbles feel smoother to the touch than either the clay or the china since they have been ground. They also usually contain fewer pits in the surface because they are made from a harder material, although this is not always a foolproof guide. If you are sorting a group which has not been handled recently you will notice that the stone marbles are colder to the touch than the clay or crockery marbles owing to the conductivity of the material. Another more damaging test involves putting a drop of acid on the marble. Limestone marbles will react to the acid and fizzing and bubbling will result where the acid touches the stone. This reaction won't occur on clay or china marbles. Also, many of the stone marbles have a flat spot somewhere on their surface. This occurs because the grinding process was not perfect, and mass production often allowed stones that weren't completely round to be included in the bags of 1,000 shipped off to the United States.

Agate

I am not sure when stone marbles made from agate were first available for boys to play with. Certainly by the last half of the 1800s agates were the marble of choice for all marble players. The reason for this is not hard to figure out. First of all, agates are beautiful. Secondly they are harder than almost all other stone marbles, and are much harder than clay, crockery or glass. Agates were always very labor intensive to produce. Thus they were never cheap and became prized possessions

Plate 1. Stone, Agate, and Semiprecious Stones.

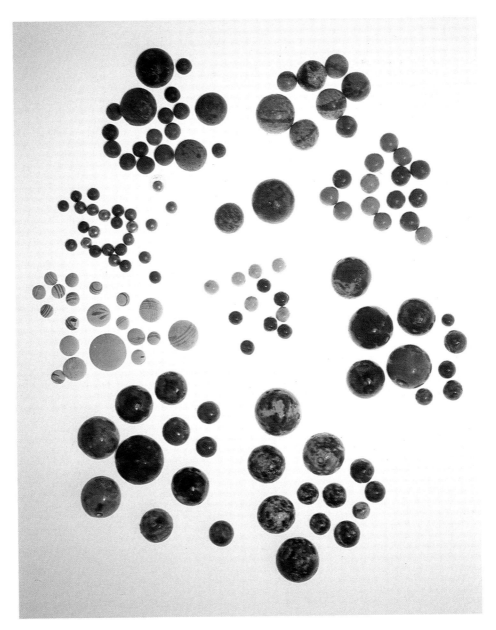

Plate 2. Clay and Benningtons.

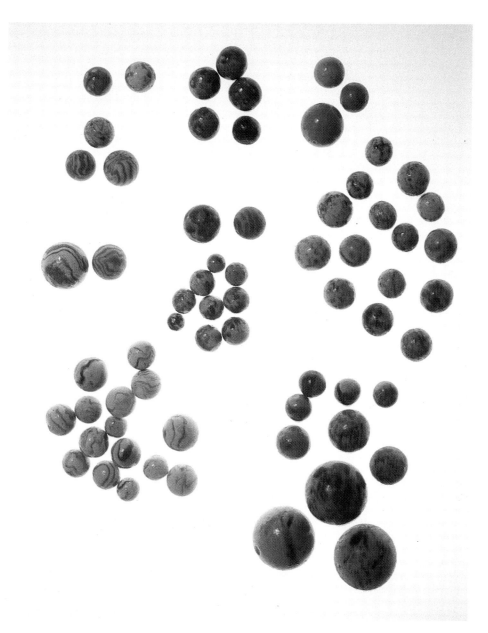

Plate 3. Crockery and Stoneware.

Plate 4. China Lines, Leaves, and Bullseyes.

Plate 5. China Flowers, Geometrics, and Scene Marble.

Plate 6. Carpet Bowls and Jacks.

Plate 7. Carpet Bowls.

Plate 8. Latticinio Cores.

Plate 9. Unusual Latticinio Cores.

Plate 10. Ridged and Column Solid Cores.

Plate 11. Unusual Solid Cores.

Plate 12. Divided Cores.

Plate 13. Ribbon Cores and Unusual Divided Cores.

Plate 14. Onionskin and Ribbon Lutz.

Plate 15. Banded Lutz: Clear, Colored, and Opaque.

Plate 16. Colored Glass with Outer Decoration.

of boys lucky enough to own one. An early article in *Harpers Young People* magazine (Roberts, 1883) refers to "the most beautiful and expensive of all marbles—the true agates and true carnelians."

Antique agates came from Germany. On the Nahe River at Obserstein, Germany there were large agates mills and quarries. The smaller pieces of stone were used to make marbles, mainly for export. Marbles were formed from the agates by skilled workmen who chipped the pieces nearly round with a hammer and then wore down the edges on the surface of a large grindstone. Agate is very hard, and the little stones were often so small they were difficult to hold tightly with one's fingers. However they were managed with great dexterity by the workmen, who in a few minutes shaped them into perfect spheres. These marble grinders worked from a horizontal position in front of vertically rotating sandstone wheels.

Agate marble production reached a peak in the Idar-Oberstein area between 1880 and 1890. At that time marbles were being ground both in Idar-Oberstein and in Bundenbach, a small town in the same region. Many of the expert agate grinders (who specialized in marbles) came from Niederworrenbach, another small town in the same region. Surprisingly enough, marbles were quite popular in Africa at this time and a great portion of them were exported there. The marbles which were produced in the greatest volume and which were the most important to the trade were those made of banded agate. However the grinders of this region also produced marbles of rose quartz, tiger eye, and other semiprecious stones.

During this period women still wore hats with large hatpins in them. These long pins were often decorated at the end with a marble of some type of stone. Marbles at this time were called "clickers" by merchants and grinders and this term is still in common use in Germany today. At the Leipzig Trade Fair, which the merchants from Idar-Oberstein regularly attended during the 19th century, clickers were sold mainly to toy merchants from the province of Thuringen. These merchants then exported them with the rest of their merchandise to North America. Agate marbles and a wide range of jewelry are still produced today in Idar-Oberstein.

Agates come in many different shades, but most can be distinguished by the bands of different colors which circle the marbles (Plate 1, left center and center). The bands usually alternate red and white, brown and white, or gray and white, although there is almost an infinite variety of shades which can be found, including black. Sometimes the bands will increase in width as they near the end of the marble forming, say, a white spot surrounded by a red band, which results in the bullseye pattern. Agate marbles having such a bullseye pattern are among the most favored by collectors, and presumably by the boys who played with them. Some of the agate marbles are much more translucent and have less well defined bands. Other agates can be recognized by small "eyes." Eyes are small circular or irregular blobs of color which are different from the overall color of the stone. These little pools of color, however, are often banded within themselves with the bands following the contour of the eye, whatever shape that might be. Again many of these marbles will be translucent or will have some part which is translucent.

Agates can be distinguished from the imitation onyx or glass marbles produced in this country by the regular bands and concentric layers of color. The imitation glass marbles usually have irregular swirls of white coloring within a matrix that is brown, green, or some other color. An agate marble which has been hit around a little will have fractures that appear inside rather than being chipped on the outside as glass marbles would be. These fractures will have the appearance of tiny round circles, similar to a piece of wax which has been stuck with a pin. As was stated before, these fractures occur within the rock and can barely be felt on the outside, if at all.

Every once in a while you may encounter a marble which appears to be agate, but is some color which no respectable agate would be found in, such as green or blue (Plate 1, upper left). Fortunately there is an easy explanation; agate is one of the semiprecious stones which can be colored either by dyeing or by heating. The finished product is really lovely since the green or blue color is not a coat on the surface but penetrates the entire marble, replacing the color which was previously present. Such marbles are just as translucent after the coloring process as they were before.

Perhaps one of the saddest aspects of marble collecting is that these beautiful and durable agates made with great effort by extremely skilled craftsmen have not appreciated the way other types of marbles have. The reason for this, too, is easy to see. New technologies in grinding and sphere making came along with the increasing popularity of gem and mineral collecting. This steadily improved the ability of gem and mineral dealers and collectors to cheaply produce marbles of agate and other types of stone. Since agates have been produced right up to the present, the price of old agates has tended to be tied down to the price of new agates, thus greatly undervaluing what should be an appreciating collectible.

Unfortunately there is no sure fire way to tell an agate made in 1890 from an agate made in 1990. The only real way to determine the age of an agate is to have historical information on it—a "paper trail" which leads you back to the original owner or to a time frame where it is fairly certain the agates would not be a reproduction.

While agates with such a history are not common, such collections do exist. As an example, there is a collection of handmade agate marbles that can be traced (with only a little uncertainty) to the mayor of Nashville in 1857. This gentleman brought these agates back from Germany. The marbles were purchased from his grandniece and have been kept in a single collection. What should these agates be worth today? A 1910 Butler Brothers catalog lists Nos. 1 and 2 agates at $2.65 for a box of 25. This same catalog on the same page lists fancy gold band glass marbles (i.e. the highly touted Lutz) at 45 cents per hundred for No. 1 and 55 cents per hundred for No. 2. So let's say that the Nos. 1 and 2 would be mixed at 50 cents per hundred. If such a Lutz now sells for at least $100 (and it does), that means it has undergone an appreciation of 20,000 times its original value of $\frac{1}{2}$ cent apiece. If the agate marbles originally priced at 10.6 cents apiece in the same catalog had undergone the same appreciation, they would now be selling for $2,120 each! Of course, this is not really a fair comparison. Current values are reflected by current rarity, which in turn is influenced by how long some of these marbles were in production. Lutz marbles probably were not produced over as long a period of time as agate marbles. Also Lutz marbles need to have sort of a pizzazz factor figured into the price. Nonetheless, agates which can be proven to be genuine handmade antiques from Germany deserve a better market than they've seen over the last couple of decades.

Before I leave the subject of agate marbles, I would like to make a few finer distinctions as to the actual types of stone referred to as agate. This is mainly for those who are rock hounds and who would be offended if I left the subject go in an unscientific manner. Agate belongs to a type of quartz called cryptocrystalline, which means that it consists of microscopic crystals, as opposed to regular quartz which has larger crystals. One big section of this group of quartz is known as chalcedony. Agate is a form of chalcedony with a banded or irregular, variegated appearance. If the agate has even, parallel layers of black and white or brown and white as some "agate" marbles do, it is no longer just agate but should be called onyx. When the bands are still even and parallel but now the colors are carnelian and white (red and white) the stone has changed names again and should be referred to as sardonyx. The term carnelian refers to another form of chalcedony that is some shade of red and is evenly colored without any banding. Now you can have all kinds of fun classifying your marbles.

Semiprecious Stones

Another type of stone made into marbles in Germany was tigereye (Plate 1, lower left). Tigereye is golden quartz with inclusions of a type of asbestos which often has blue fibers. This stone is not mined in Germany itself but comes from such unlikely places as Griqualand West, South Africa. Tigereye marbles appear to be dark brown in color with bright golden bands circling them. When the marble is rotated these bands will shift position, running up and down the marble as the angle of light changes. This effect is caused by the asbestos fibers inside the quartz reflecting the light, and the type of pattern shown on any particular marble depends upon how the fibers are lined up inside it. Sometimes the blue of the asbestos can be seen, giving parts of the marble a bluish cast. These marbles come in approximately the same size range as do the agate marbles, since they were produced in the same manner.

Rose quartz marbles were also made by the early German craftsmen and are fairly easy to identify by their pink color (Plate 1, lower right). Most pieces of rose quartz of any size are fractured inside, since even the natural stone before grinding is seldom perfect. Therefore many rose quartz marbles will show cracks or fractures which may not even reach the surface. These were not caused by hard use, but were probably present when the marble was first ground.

Another stone which was used occasionally to produce marbles was the bloodstone (Plate 1, on right, above rose quartz). This is a form of green chalcedony (that quartz with the microscopic crystals again) with red spots scattered through it resembling drops of blood. The green color of the stone is often quite dark, being almost a blue-green in shade. With such a background the small specks of red contrast quite brightly.

Another imported stone which was occasionally made into a marble was the opal (Plate 1, lower center). Opals, like rose quartz, would have been expensive even when they were first produced, since the stone had to be imported and was quite vulnerable to cracking under the heat of the grinding process. Since very few rose quartz, bloodstone, or opal marbles were produced, all of these types are quite rare today. However, as with agates, these types of stones are presently being made into marbles by sphere machines, and having a history is very important.

I have seen a few marbles made from still other types of stone than those already mentioned. One is red with a yellowish white patch and is probably a form of jasper. Two others appear to be some form of quartz, probably a poorer grade of agate. One resembles the bacon agate type of stone which is prevalent along Lake Superior at Michigan's upper peninsula. Often it is hard to identify a particular type of stone from which a marble has been made, even if you are a rock hound and have a fair degree of familiarity with the different varieties of gemstones. The two crucial points are to be sure that the marble is of stone and not glass or crockery, and to be sure that the marble is old.

There are several tests to check the composition—some have been mentioned in the limestone and agate sections. Certainly, any bubbles inside the marble will indicate glass. You could also look at the marble with a magnifying glass under reasonably good light. Check the highlight of the lamp bulb on the marble through the magnifying glass. If the marble is of stone it will have been ground and you should be able to see fine parallel lines at some spots on the marble. Many marbles have fine lines all over the surface which can readily be seen by the method described. Finally, some of the stone marbles were never ground perfectly round, and if looked at under a magnifying glass will appear to be more a series of small flat spots than a sphere. Be careful though: the workmanship on some was much better than this, making the first two tests more reliable than this one. Once composition has been established, you'll want to try to date the marble, thereby determining its value. If the marble has no history the odds are it is a recent marble made by a gemstone enthusiast, and has no more value than if purchased new.

Once again as in my first edition, I'll close this chapter with a favorite of mine, a large Petoskey stone marble (Plate 1, bottom center). The name Petoskey comes from the city of Petoskey, Michigan. These stones are only found along Lake Michigan from Petoskey to Charlevoix, with the exceptions of some similar types which are found in southern Iowa and southern Indiana. Petoskey stone is a type of fossilized coral, or to be more specific, a calcite replaced coral of the genus *Hexagonaria*. The genus name *Hexagonaria* refers to the fact that the coral cells of this group are six sided. Therefore, the fossil stones display a pattern of little hexagons one next to the other across the surface. The marble is light brown in color and is over $2\frac{1}{4}''$ in diameter, although not a perfect sphere. The six sided pattern is shown on both ends of the sphere, with light brown outlining the darker brown cell interior. Between the poles of the marble where the cells have been cut lengthwise, parallel lines can be seen traveling down from the center of each cell. This marble would be a collector's item as a fossil specimen if nothing else, since specimens of this size with a clear pattern are hard to find. This marble is classed as an antique only because I know the history of it, and that it pre-dates the sphere machines used to create such things today. I would assume, however, from the type of stone, that it was ground in this country, and it was either one of a kind or one of a few and not a production item.

○2○
Clay, Crockery, and China

Clay

Clay or earthenware marbles, like stone marbles, probably have a very ancient lineage. They had already reached North America long before the American revolution. Archaeologists have found marbles at Fort Albany on James Bay in Canada. Fort Albany was a fur trading post run by the Hudson Bay Company between 1675 and 1720 (Randall, 1979). Although the marbles at Fort Albany were undoubtedly made in Europe, clay marbles were later manufactured in the United States. The earliest American manufacturer of clay marbles for which we have records was the Frazey Pottery in Zanesville, Ohio (Randall, 1979). This pottery produced the locally famous (and probably locally distributed) "Frazey's Clays" in 1818–1819 (Carskadden et al., 1985). Presumably when the pottery closed, Mr. Frazey wandered north and a little west and founded the town of Frazeysburg, about 16 miles from Zanesville as the crow flies. He must have been a busy man! Unfortunately, no known examples of Frazey's Clays exist.

Factories which produced marbles as a major product for sale were fairly common by the turn of the century. As many as eleven factories may have been producing clay marbles in northeastern Ohio alone (Carskadden et al., 1985), although many of these produced other products such as electrical porcelain as well. The first of these northeastern Ohio factories for which we have records was founded by Samuel C. Dyke in Akron, Ohio in 1884 (Stoat, 1923). He was soon producing 30,000 marbles a day. Another factory was started by A.L. Dyke, also in Akron, in 1889. In about 1890 the two Dykes consolidated their factories (actually a group of Akron investors bought them both out) and the American Marble and Toy Manufacturing Company emerged from the union (Carskadden et al., 1985). Products from this company, which was in business between 1890 and 1904, were nationally advertised in the Montgomery Ward 1895 catalog (Carskadden and Gartley, 1990). Competition came from the J.F. Brown Company in Akron which was founded in 1895 and was soon producing 100,000 marbles a day. The Lightcap and Allbright Company set up an original factory in Ravenna, Ohio, then later established a second factory at Limaville, Ohio. The story of this latter factory was told to me by Earl Fasnaught, who was born in Limaville in 1893 and grew up there.

In 1893 an old German pottery factory was located in Limaville. This was operated by a Mr. Kuntze and his sons with other employees from the immediate area. The location of the factory was next to the tracks of the Cleveland and Pittsburgh railroad, a division of the Pennsylvania railroad west of Pittsburgh. This location proved to be disastrous. After several large fires blamed on the passing trains, most of the plant was destroyed except for the kilns. The site stood idle for some time, then was purchased by the Lightcap and Allbright Company from Ravenna.

This company then proceeded to rebuild the plant. The old kilns were revamped to suit their needs and new machinery to be used in the manufacture of clay marbles was brought in and set up. One of the new machines ground the clay. Another was a wad cutter used to cut the clay after it had been properly processed into wads. These small cut wads were then placed into long wooden drums suspended diagonally on power-driven line shafts. These drums rolled the wads until they were round. During this process the wads were hardened and made firmer due to the high temperature of the area they were in. Next the marbles were placed into the kilns in saugers (vessels made of fire clay) where they were fired to complete the process of hardening. For the first few years these kilns were fired with wood but later soft coal was used for this purpose.

When the marbles were removed from the kilns they were placed in long wooden cylinders and dyed. This completed the manufacturing process. The marbles were then inspected, graded, and placed in small cloth sacks for shipment to various stores, especially the five-and-ten-cent stores. After enjoying a very healthy business for some time, the plant suffered a disastrous fire (again blamed on passing trains). That marked the end of the clay marble production in Limaville, since no other similar factory has since been constructed in the town. This final fire occurred sometime between 1906 and 1910.

Clay marbles continued to be produced into the era of machine-made marbles. They were advertised as late as 1928, when they appeared in the Sears Roebuck catalog. An article by Wilbur Stout written in 1923 concludes with this comment on the clay marble business in Ohio: "the business has not prospered for many years in this country owing to importation of large quantities from foreign sources, especially from Germany which has good clays and cheap labor." Unfortunately for clay marble manufacturers, long before World War II eliminated the German market, machine-made marbles had been perfected in both quality and price to the point that handmade clay marbles could no longer compete.

Clay or earthenware marbles were fired at a lower temperature than other types of ceramic marbles. They were called commies by children because they were the common marble to play with (Plate 2, upper left). Many commies are the colors of the original clay: tans, reds, and browns. Others have been decorated with different kinds of paints or designs. Brightly dyed solid colored clay marbles were made in the plants around Akron near the turn of the century. These include marbles of the Allbright brand which were made at the plants spoken of earlier at Ravenna and Lima, Ohio. It is not known at what particular time painted clays first started to be made nor is it known whether all of the natural earth tone clays are older than the painted commies (probably not). Solid colored painted clays with a metallic finish (Plate 2, left above center) were used in a game called Gloria Mosaic which will be discussed in Chapter 8. Occasionally one will find clays heavily painted with a single color (Plate 2, upper right) and very rarely examples speckled with multiple colors (Plate 2, upper center). The latter speckled clays were produced earlier than most clay marbles and were originally called "birds eggs." Roberts (1883) in his article "Marbles and Where They Come From" describes clay marbles in "a style speckled with various colored points, which are called 'birds eggs.'"

Another distinctive group are the clays having lines of paint either running in circles or in a wobbly coil, or in crisscrossing wobbly lines (Plate 2, top right). Once again Akron comes into the picture. Matthew Lang, who lived in Akron, developed a patent for rolling marbles down a series of trays with color to produce this sort of a pattern. Thus these marbles are referred to as rolled commies since the rolling gives them their distinctive color pattern. Given the wide range of factories and long time period over which these marbles were made, more distinctive types will probably become evident as collectors gain renewed interest in this area and look at these marbles with more discrimination. Commies, after all, are very appealing. They were the marbles most often played with in the past and can still be purchased at a relatively low price. There is something to be said about collecting real workhorse marbles rather than marbles that were produced primarily for show.

All sizes are represented in clay marbles, although smaller sizes are more common. Sizes comparing with the large German swirls or sulphides (i.e. sizes above about $1\frac{1}{2}''$) are very rare. The reason for this is apparent. As stated previously these were cheap common marbles manufactured for children to play with. Since children seldom played with marbles greater than $1''$ in diameter, it stands to reason that few clay manufacturers would have bothered to make such a large marble. The shape of these marbles is also quite varied. Many are oblong or flat sided. It is tempting to think that some of the more crudely shaped marbles were produced in earlier times by cruder production methods, but that is difficult to prove. These marbles often contain chips or other damage, which is to be expected, since again they were the marbles most often played with by children around the turn of the last century. Commies in good condition were probably never played with or at least played with very little.

Another type of marble which fits under the heading of earthenware (marbles fired at low temperatures) was referred to as unglazed china or porcelain in my previous edition. This term isn't really accurate since true unglazed china or porcelain is much harder and fired at higher temperatures. These marbles were, however, made of kaolin, a fine white clay which was also used in the manufacture of china marbles. Kaolin is used medically for the treatment of diarrhea. I assume there is no direct connection between the medicinal use of kaolin and the fact that some of these marbles have been found in archaeological excavations of privies. These marbles are also called pipe clay marbles by some collectors, since the pipes used as a major trade item with Indians in North America were also made from kaolin. The early voyagers, who liked to smoke pipes, used them to figure out how far they had traveled in a given day. About each hour the voyagers would quit paddling and smoke a pipe. Therefore they measured their travel in terms of the number of pipes it took them.

These low-fired kaolin or pipe clay marbles can be distinguished from unglazed ceramic marbles by their chalky appearance (they were referred to as "chalkies" by marble players), and by the fact that they will absorb water easily because they are porous. For the same reason the color patterns on these marbles will often smear if rubbed with a damp cloth. Pipe clay marbles were produced towards the end of the time period in which clay marbles were made. They may have been made as early as the 1890s but most were probably produced in the early 1900s. Most of them appear to have been painted and decorated in a hurry (Plate 2, left center). Instead of painting parallel lines or concentric circles, which would be time consuming, the decorator simply put his or her paint brush on the marble and gave the marble a spin. This resulted in a coil or helix pattern. Often pastel colors were used, which are unlike those used on the regular glazed china marbles. Most of these pipe clay marbles were probably produced in Germany.

Crockery

Many of the crockery or stoneware marbles, particularly those with a brown or blue glaze, have been called Bennington marbles by dealers and collectors because of their similarity to the brown and blue glazed Bennington pottery ware. In order to see if the name was correct I contacted the Bennington Museum in Bennington, Vermont. Their reply stated that the Rockingham potteries at Bennington did not manufacture marbles as a production item. Subsequent research (Carskadden et al., 1985) has indicated that Rockingham potteries in other parts of the country (such as the one at East Liverpool, Ohio) did not produce these marbles either. Although it is entirely possible the individual workmen made marbles for their own children there is no way to know whether this was done or not. Even if it was, this would scarcely account for any significant percentage of the large numbers of these marbles which are still in existence today. On the contrary, many private collectors have in their possession boxes of the original marbles clearly marked "Made in Germany." This not only indicates the German origin but also indicates a post-1890 date of production. It was in 1890 that the McKinley Tariff Act was written requiring the "Made in Germany" stamp to be put on such exported materials.

These marbles were produced by the same techniques used to make other pieces of pottery. Small pieces of clay were shaped into spheres and then the spheres were coated with glaze and fired. The two most common glazes were a manganese glaze which created a brown color and a cobalt glaze which created a blue color. These were the only two readily available glazes which could stand up under the higher temperatures used to produce stoneware. Many of these marbles were not perfect spheres, showing that they were produced in large numbers without much time being wasted on workmanship or quality control. These marbles are also characterized by eyes which are present on the surface. An eye is a small circular spot with very little or no glaze on it surrounded by a thick ring of glaze which may be heavy enough to appear almost black. These eyes represent the places where the marble either touched other marbles or the support surface in the kiln where it was fired.

Even though our knowledge of the locations and times of production of crockery factories are much less complete than even those of the clay factories, we can assume these marbles were made by a variety of factories over a number of years. The three most common types of what might be called the Bennington sub-group of crockery marbles are the brown Benningtons, blue Benningtons, and fancy Benningtons. Brown glazed marbles are by far the most common of the three (Plate 2, lower left). These marbles come in a wide variety of shades and intensity of the glaze. At one extreme are marbles which are dark brown with even darker, almost black marks which give them a mottled appearance. The glaze on these marbles is often very thick and shiny. At the other extreme are some light tan marbles with a barely noticeable glaze. Of course all kinds of intermediate color shades exist. Most of these marbles have a distinct mottled appearance and none of them is ever the same shade of brown over the entire marble. Whether the different color types and glaze thickness were produced at different factories or whether they were just in different batches from the same factory is difficult to say.

The blue Benningtons (Plate 2, center right) also vary in the depth of color and intensity of glaze with which they were produced. Many of these marbles also have a markedly mottled appearance. Dark blue, light blue, and white areas can be found on the same marble. In general, however, they do not show quite as great a variety of types as do the brown glazed marbles. Fancy Benningtons have both blue and brown markings and often quite a bit of white too (Plate 2, lower right). From the number of these which exist and from the combination of distinct blue and brown it can be safely assumed that they were produced separately and with some more work than was spent on the others. The color on these marbles ranges from those which are almost completely white to those which are a mass of blue and brown markings. Fancy Benningtons are less common than the blue Bennington and much less common than the brown Bennington. In all three of these Benningtons large marbles 1″ or more in diameter are much less common than smaller shooting size marbles. As with the clays, these marbles were mass-produced probably, hitting their peak in the 1890s as inexpensive playing marbles for children. Thus few very large Benningtons were made since children did not routinely play with such a large marble.

One indication that the wide range of Bennington color shades may represent marbles made at different factories comes from some research done in Zanesville, Ohio (Carskadden et al., 1985). Starting in the late 1820s a range of stoneware pottery was manufactured in the Zanesville area (Schneider, 1957). One type using a lead glaze and called "yellow ware" was produced as early as 1846 by Housen and Hallam. By 1848 this factory was making Bennington-type ware. Housen and Hallam manufactured yellow ware ink wells from the early 1860s to about 1874 (Everhart, 1882). Limited excavation of a dump site near the pottery produced one of the yellow ware ink wells as well as a yellow ware unglazed marble. The brown line design on this marble suggests that it was in imitation of the porcelain marbles being imported from Germany. A number of undecorated yellow ware marbles have been found in Zanesville privies and are also suspected to have been produced by Housen and Hallam. Unfortunately these marbles look very much like the light tan Bennington marbles. In fact, they seem to be indistinguishable from the types that traditionally have been grouped with brown Benningtons. Obviously more research is needed to be able to distinguish those marbles made by different companies which had similar manufacturing processes.

In my first edition I mentioned that some of the fancy Benningtons showed some pink color. However it wasn't until I compared my collection with that of Jeff Carskadden that it became apparent that these were a distinctive type of marble. On a mildly historic day in September of 1989 Jeff Carskadden, unarguably the world's authority on ceramic marbles, and I brought our collections together and spread them out across the floor. Often it is only when two or three large collections are brought together that you can determine the status of those marbles which closely resemble a known type, but seem to have some consistent difference from it. If such marbles are very rare, any one collector has so few that it is impossible to determine whether they are the result of an occasional accident in the production process, or whether you have a representative of an extremely rare group that was deliberately produced. Jeff's sampling of fancy pink Benningtons together with mine proved that they were a production item and not a quality control problem. Thus fancy pink Benningtons (or fancy pinks) now have to stand on their own as another sub-group of Bennington marbles (Plate 3, lower center). They were certainly produced by the same methods that produced the other Bennington types, and may have even been produced at the same factories. The pink on these marbles is spotty and almost looks as if it was a powder that was dusted on or some sort of a spray. However it was applied, the fancy pinks are definitely a pretty marble and well worth having in a collection. However, judging from the size of my collection and Jeff's collection and the number of fancy pinks that we own, my guess is that these are extremely rare marbles, at least as compared to other Bennington types.

There are two other groups of marbles that belong in the Bennington sub-group, both of which are extremely rare. One of these, which was also identified by Jeff and me at our joint meeting, is a patched Bennington. These marbles have distinctive areas or patches of green, brown and blue (Plate 3, upper center). The fact that these colors are not intermixed over the entire surface but occur in separate well-defined areas demonstrate this marble was made differently than other Benningtons. I believe this technique is sufficiently different to indicate these marbles were at least produced in a different factory (if not in a different county) than regular Bennington marbles. Again, judging by how few there are in our joint collections, patched Benningtons should be considered extremely rare.

One final sub-group of the Bennington type are pink or lavender (Plate 3, upper right) or green (Plate 3, upper center) glazed Benningtons. Those that I have seen are all fairly small in size, but their distinctive solid color pattern in some shade of green or pink leaning towards lavender sets them apart from the other crockery marbles. Again these were made as a production item although probably in small quantities. They were either a limited run of a glaze that in the final analysis was too expensive or too difficult to use, or they were a test market of a color which never caught on. Under either of those scenarios they would have been produced for a short time, and would be extremely rare today. Some early catalogs mention American majolica marbles. Since majolica often has these same pink, lavender, and green colors, it is tempting to assume that these were the marbles so named.

Another type of crockery marble quite distinctive from the Bennington varieties has been referred to as lined crockery, although variegated stoneware might be a better name. Most of this type are white with blue or green or blue *and* green lines running around the marble (Plate 3, lower left). Actually the lines run through the marble. These marbles were made by taking clays of different colors and then mixing or swirling them together one into the other. Thus the lines of color go all the way through the center of the marble, as can be seen by cutting one open. (Not that I recommend this research technique for collectors.) One would expect that the colors would be smudged together on the outside of a piece of clay that had been shaped into a sphere. Since they are not, some technique must have been used to either cut the marbles into the round shape or to grind them down later to eliminate the smudged areas.

These marbles have had a long history, being found in pre-1850 privies in Cincinnati (Grist and Grist, 1983) and in privies elsewhere dating from the 1870s to 1892 (Carskadden et al., 1985). They are mentioned as early as 1829 in *The Boys' Own Book* as "Dutch-variegated clay—the cheapest" (Carskadden and Gartley, 1990A). Roberts' (1883) article in *Harpers Young People* mentions these marbles as follows: "Next come the jaspers, or, as the boys call them, 'Croton alleys,' consisting of glazed and unglazed white china handsomely marbled with blue." Thus both the glazed and unglazed marbles were produced at the same time. The vast majority of these marbles have both green and blue lines in the same marble. Marbles having only two colors of clay are very rare. These include blue and white, green and white, and especially pink and white (Plate 3, left, center to bottom). Pink is rare in any color combination. Also rare are marbles having something other than white as the primary color. One of these has a primarily blue base with green clay lines in it. Another has a primarily green base with blue lines in it (Plate 3, left top corner).

Another group of marbles superficially resembling the latter are best termed spattered crockery marbles. These marbles have spots of green and blue colors scattered over a white base (Plate 3, right center). However they are not made from differently colored clays but are made more like the Bennington marbles. The color is entirely on the surface. These were marketed as jaspies or china marbles and are found in boxes marked "Made in Germany," again indicating that they were produced after 1890. They appear to be an imitation of the variegated clay marbles talked about in the last paragraph. Variegated clays were early imitations of stone marbles such as jasper, thus spattered crockery marbles are a cheap imitation of a more expensive and well done imitation. They must have seen a relatively limited production time, since they are much less common today than the brown or even the blue Bennington marble.

A final category of crockery marbles might be referred to as salt glazed stoneware, even though it is not known whether all or even most of these actually were produced using a salt glaze. In some early kilns salt was used as a glaze for pottery. Throwing the salt into the kiln would vaporize it and the salt would form a glaze and give the object a sort of rough, orange peel-like texture. These marbles usually have a basic gray color and are sometimes decorated with blue (Plate 3, bottom right). The blue is a cobalt glaze that might be applied with a sponge type applicator or as a blue coil (Plate 3, upper center and Plate 5, center right) or as a blue band around the marble. North American potteries were making stoneware, salt glazed jugs and other items in the latter half of the 19th century. It is logical to assume that these marbles were produced by some of these same potteries. However, judging from their scarcity, production numbers seem to have been limited and distribution seems to have been largely local.

China

China or porcelain marbles represent the pinnacle of ceramic marble art. They have quite a long history; in the last third of the 18th century china factories rose in South Thuringen which became part of East Germany after World War II. By the turn of the 19th century some of these factories specialized in the production of china marbles. These marbles also used the fine white kaolin clay as a base. A hand-worked porcelain mass was forced through tubes, and then cut into small equal size pieces. These pieces were placed in plaster molds with long oval grooves. Through a rapid rotary motion these forms molded the porcelain pieces into spheres. The spheres were then fired at high temperature in kilns. After they had cooled they were painted in various designs, then refired at lower temperatures to set the paint. Those that were glazed had the glaze applied prior to the first firing. The pigments could not stand such high temperatures and thus were painted on top of the glaze before the second firing. When the paints were applied to the glaze rather than to the body of the marble itself they tended to fuse less completely with the surface. Thus glazed china marbles often tended to lose their decorations more quickly than the older unglazed china marbles. Note the largest flower decorated china in Plate 5 (lower left). A portion (upper right) of that marble was missed by the glaze, and the part of the flower that was painted on the unglazed portion is much clearer than the rest of the flower, which was painted on top of the glaze.

Although the Thuringen Museum indicates that china marbles were produced in Germany in the early 1800s, the first archaeological evidence we have of such marbles in North America comes from a privy in Zanesville dating between 1840 and 1850. Decorated china marbles were also recovered from two other Zanesville privies at levels dated 1850 to 1860. Similarly decorated china marbles were also found in privies and cisterns in New Orleans dated to this same time period (1850–1860) (Gartley and Carskadden, 1987). Another example now in the Royal Ontario Museum was found at Fort La Clachoe, a Hudson Bay trading post which operated between 1850 and 1870 (Randall, 1979). The first advertisement known for china marbles in the U.S. is in an 1876 Zanesville paper. Advertisements in Montgomery Ward and Sears catalogs began in 1886 and continued until 1903. A 1910 Butler Brothers catalog does mention a bag which contained a mixture of marbles including "five painted china alleys" along with a mixture of glass and clay marbles (Carskadden et al., 1985). The packaging of these marbles as part of a mixed group might have been an attempt to sell outdated or out of production stock. China marbles also became scarce in archaeological assemblages after 1900.

Recent information has revealed that very early (1840s) china marbles were produced in the United States in the Ohio River town of Troy, Indiana (Carskadden and Gartley, 1990B). English Staffordshire potter Jabez Vodrey came to the Indiana Pottery Company at Troy in 1839 and was soon put in charge. Vodrey kept a diary which survived along with his account book. Information from this material was supplied to Carskadden and Gartley by Diana and J. Garrison Stradling. As early as December 15, 1944, Vodrey records shipping 950 pipes, 9 dozen "carpet balls," 1,500 "potter(y) marbles" and 800 "china" marbles. Prices were $37\frac{1}{2}$ cents per dozen for carpet balls, $37\frac{1}{2}$ cents per hundred for pottery marbles, and $62\frac{1}{2}$ cents per hundred for china marbles. Other similar entries for shipments occur in 1844 and through 1845. An entry on February 25, 1846 details the shipment of "800 Painted Chines (Chinas)" along with six carpet balls. Although the term "painted" had not previously been used in the diary for marbles, the account book indicates that Vodrey sold hand-painted pipes at least as early as 1845. Carskadden and Gartley (1990 B) conclude that it is likely Vodrey produced the German style decorated chinas. In 1847 Vodrey left Indiana and established a new pottery at East Liverpool, Ohio. However his diary from this later period contains no mention of the production of marbles.

Many different types of decorations were used in china marbles. The styles of some of these decorations can be used to date the marble to the earlier (1850–1970) or later periods of china marble production. Although I will discuss the different designs individually, remember that they were used in combination on most marbles, and that a variety of different combinations exist. Serious collectors of china marbles should invest in a copy of Carskadden and Gartley (1990 B), which details the more unusual chinas and provides good discussion of reproductions. Pigments used for these designs include green, black, red or orange, and blue.

One of the most popular designs was a group of parallel lines or bands that would encircle the marble (Plate 4, lower right). Often two groups of lines were used which would intersect each other at right angles forming little squares or diamond patterns in the middle of the marble. The parallel lines are almost always of the same color within a group. However, different groups of parallel lines on the same marble which intersect each other are often different colors. Marbles with such a lined motif were made throughout the period of manufacture of china marbles. However, marbles having one wide band bordered by one or two parallel lines have been found in the early 1850–1860 archaeological digs (Carskadden and Gartley, 1990).

A design superficially resembling that created by parallel lines is that created by a helix or coil (Plate 4, top center and left). Helixes or coils are formed by placing the brush against the marble and then turning the marble to form a spiral pattern. If such a pattern appears in the center of a marble it is referred to as a helix. If it occurs at the end of a marble it is referred to as a coil or spiral. Coils and helixes often have a thicker dose of paint at the beginning of the line when the brush was first placed down. Of course, the paint is also continuous from one line or circle to the next, in contrast to marbles with true parallel lines or concentric circles. Although some helix marbles have been found in the early period of porcelain production they become much more common towards the later period (Carskadden and Gartley, 1990 A). Helixes appear to be a shortcut method for drawing the equivalent of parallel lines or concentric circles. Some marbles are densely covered with a series of differently colored intersecting helixes. They appear to be a separate production item, and have been referred to as plaid marbles because of their distinctive appearance (Plate 4, top center group, lower left).

Bullseyes were another popular design on china marbles. Three different types of bullseyes were painted during three different manufacturing periods. One style had a solid dot or eye at its center (Plate 4, center column, second from bottom). Another consisted of a broad ring resembling a donut (Plate 4, center column third and fourth from bottom). A third type was produced by a series of thin or narrow concentric rings (Plate 4, upper right). The solid eye and donut varieties were produced between 1850 and 1890. Some of the concentric ring bullseyes, especially those with four or more rings, also date from this early period. However concentric ring bullseyes having two or three rings were only manufactured in the 1890s and early 1900s and are the only ones pictured in trade merchandise catalogs from the turn of the century (Carskadden and Gartley, 1990 A).

Leaves or "turkey tracks" are a common design on china marbles, and are almost always used in combination with other designs. Leaves can occur as alternating left and right brush strokes forming a wreath around the marble or they can occur as a group or spray of leaves. Although green is the most common color for the leaf brush strokes other colors are seen as well. Rarely three or four leaves will radiate from a stem forming a shamrock or four leaf clover design (Plate 5, inner circle, upper left). An early pattern consists of a marble having two circles which intersect at right angles. These quarter the marble and divide it into four sections. Inside each of the sections is a series of leaves (Plate 5, upper right). More common is a coil with leaves on the other end (Plate 4, left column, second from top). These probably date from the 1890s. Also occurring are coils on either end with leaves in the middle and leaves on either end with a coil or helix in the middle (Plate 4, left column, third from top). A much rarer marble has two doughnut bullseyes on either end with leaves circling the center of the marble (Plate 4, center bottom).

Sometimes four to thirteen of the leaf brush strokes radiate out from the central point or dot forming a geometric pattern (Plate 5, upper left). Such a design is referred to as a daisy wheel. A common pattern for these uncommon marbles is to have two daisy wheels, one at either end, usually with a series of parallel lines around the center of the marble. The leaves or petals on any individual daisy wheel are usually of the same color. However rare examples exist of two colors being used, such as the red and green wheels in the upper left portion of Plate 5. Almost all colors have been used for the daisy wheels. Usually the two daisy wheels on the single marble are the same color, although not always. Daisy wheels date from the early part of the china marble production period being found in privies dating from 1850–1860 (Carskadden et al., 1985). This design is not found in later archaeological sites nor is it shown in turn-of-the-century catalogs (Carskadden and Gartley, 1990 A).

Flowers represent perhaps not only the most beautiful design used on china marbles but the one having the most variations. Early flower patterns include two versions which resemble the early bullseyes only with a stem and leaves. These are a solid dot or "tomato," or "apple" flower and a doughnut-shaped flower (Plate 5, top right). These designs date from the 1850s–1860s. Slightly later, from perhaps the mid-period of production, is a King's rose, an open rose design that appears to have a touch of Pennsylvania Dutch in it (Plate 5, lower right). Also from the mid to late period starting in the 1870s are the pink roses or pinkies (Plate 5, lower right, left of open rose). These are still made with a great deal of care and are very beautiful. Other flowers made later in the period from 1890–1910 are done more hurriedly using fewer brush strokes (Plate 5, bottom and lower left). All flower motifs are rare with those produced earliest found least often. While most flowers are in red, some also occur in blue or even as a two-toned blue and red. Occasionally early (1850–1870) marbles will have a wreath around the center consisting of green leaves and a series of red or blue dots (Plate 5, lower right, below blue swirl) (Gartley and Carskadden, 1987). These polychromed stenciled or dot flowers are very rare. Such dot flowers may also occur individually (Plate 5, top right, inner circle). Finally there are some china marbles which are almost covered with large floral designs. These designs are often abstract, sometimes appearing to be tulips. In fact these marbles have quite a Pennsylvania Dutch character to them. The age of these marbles is not known, but they are believed to be authentic antiques and not reproductions.

The rarest of all china marbles are those having a scene with people or animals painted around the center of the marble. Usually these marbles have a daisy wheel at either end. To my knowledge only eleven of these marbles are known or rumored to exist. The scenes on two of these marbles include a man and a woman with a sailing boat in the background, although the scenes are not identical. Other paintings include a dog, a man on a stump with a pipe, a horse and carriage, a cottage, a hunting scene, a man plowing a field with a horse, a man riding a horse, a man viewing a castle up on a rock, and a boy in a wheat field drinking from a flask. These marbles range from $1\frac{1}{8}''$ to $1\frac{3}{4}''$ in diameter. The scenes contain a variety of colors and the daisy wheels on different marbles may be differently colored. Some of the daisy wheels on these scene marbles don't start at a central point but radiate from the outer ring of a solid dot bullseye. Daisy wheels are often separated from the scene by a single line encircling the marble. At this time we do not know when or where these marbles were produced, although the daisy wheel motif would seem to place them in the early 1850s–1860s (Carskadden and Gartley, 1990 A). They were obviously not a mass production item, instead being something produced in limited quantities, perhaps for a special event such as a centennial or exposition.

That they are unlikely to be modern reproductions is borne out by the way I obtained my marble of the man sitting on the stump smoking his pipe (Plate 5, center). A student who had been in one of my courses when I was a teaching assistant at the University of Wisconsin in Madison had a younger brother who was working during the summer cleaning out storm sewers for the city of Beloit, Wisconsin. In the mud at the bottom of one of these storm sewers he found this marble. His sister remembered that I had a marble collection, and brought it in to show me. At the time (1972) I had never seen or heard of anything like it, and I purchased it from her. It is unlikely that a reproduction would wind up in a storm sewer in Beloit, Wisconsin, especially since at that time these marbles had no particular value. So just remember, if you think that rare marbles are too expensive for you to afford, there is always a chance that something nice may pop up out of your local storm sewer.

The count of marbles collected over the years by my father and myself provides some idea of the relative rarity of the major types of china marbles (Table 2-1). Intersecting helixes are far and away the most common variety, making up almost $\frac{1}{3}$ of the total. This design is almost $2\frac{1}{2}$ times more common than the earlier design it replaced, that of intersecting parallel lines. Also fairly common are the later style of thin bullseyes with multiple concentric rings, and leaves either alone or in conjunction with a coil or double coil or helix. Single or double non-intersecting coils, or a single helix with no other decoration are relatively uncommon, probably because these designs were felt to be too simple and unattractive to be very salable.

More uncommon yet are the earlier style doughnut or solid bullseye marble, even when grouped together with and without leaf decorations. Rarest of all are geometrics, flowers and other extremely unusual designs such as scenes or thunderbirds or eagles. All of these lumped together comprise only 4% of the total. You can imagine what sort of percentages would result if we separated these into sub-categories. This is why many collectors own and display marbles in the latter categories which are faded or damaged to a point that would result in other types of antique marbles being thrown into the trash bin. Marbles of such rarity are hard to come by in any condition, and can enhance a collection even when faded.

TABLE 2-1   RELATIVE RARITY (%) OF CHINA MARBLES BY DESIGN (SAMPLE SIZE = 248)

Intersecting helixes	32%
Non-intersecting coils or helixes	6%
Leaves alone or with coil or helix	18%
Thin bullseyes	21%
Intersecting parallel lines	13%
Doughnut or solid bullseyes, with or without leaves	5%
Geometrics, flowers, and other	4%

3

Carpet Bowls

Carpet bowls or balls are brightly colored, hand-decorated ceramic spheres sought after by collectors, particularly collectors of antique marbles. Many collectors have a few carpet bowls in their collections and most carpet bowl collectors collect marbles as well. I am pleased to be able to give carpet bowls a well deserved chapter of their own, largely with information graciously supplied by collector John Moore. The terms "balls" and "bowls" seem to be used somewhat interchangeably today, and both can be found in the earlier literature. However the term bowls seems to be the older of the two, and so to be consistent I will try to use it in the rest of the chapter.

History and Rules of Game

Carpet bowls are related to, but different from, both lawn bowls and marbles. Marbles, as we have already discussed, is an ancient game, and sculptured vases and plaques exist that indicate a form of lawn bowls or bowling on the green was played at least 3,500 to 4,000 years ago (Menke, 1953). The form of carpet bowling in which the spheres now being collected were used can be traced back to 1796, when we have a known founding date for Thomas Taylor Bowls Limited of

Glasgow, Scotland. In the late 1800s many well-to-do Scots spent the majority of their Sunday afternoons playing carpet bowls. The game could be played either outside on a carpet or inside in a hallway or parlor or drawing room. One antiques dealer in Edinborough told me that most of the old Scottish mansions had two boxes inside the door in the hallway, one of these contained a croquet set and the other a set of carpet bowls. Thus carpet bowls and croquet were both genteel diversions for the upper class in the Victorian era.

However the game survived well into the 1900s and managed to cross the Atlantic and take root in Canada (Biernacki, 1984). From the 1910s into the 1950s carpet bowling was one of the social activities sponsored by several of the churches in Canada. United, Baptist, and Anglican churches all sponsored carpet bowling leagues. Most parishes sponsored one team and some sponsored two. Teams played once a week within their own league, but little inter-league play occurred. Such league play has now all but disappeared, and carpet bowling as a sport has become largely relegated to a few senior citizen centers.

Rules for carpet bowling changed slightly from time to time and place to place. The following are rules put out by the Henselite Company, a later maker of non-ceramic carpet bowls, and distributed out of Margesson's Sports Limited, a now defunct sports shop located in Toronto.

1. The Carpet (Fig. 3-1) shall be 48″ by 30′ and be marked as follows: From spot to spot, 21′ 6″. Center circle, 10″ in diameter. Middle circle, 6″ beyond and around the center circle. Outer circle, 6″ beyond and around the middle circle.

2. Lines must be $\frac{1}{2}$″ in thickness. This means the counting space of center ring is 9″ and the other two circles only $5\frac{1}{2}$″.

3. Scoring points for games: Inner Circle, 3 points; Middle Circle 2 points; Outer Circle 1 point. By standing directly above the ball, the circle line must be visible before points are allowed. A ball not clear of the outer edge of line of circle counts in next circle.

4. Balls running 6″ beyond circles are dead. Hog-lines are 15″ in front of circles. Balls in play that do not go over the "hog-line" are removed from carpet.

5. Games consist of six players on each side, three of each side at each end and playing 2 balls each, alternately.

Fig. 3-1. Carpet Bowl court.

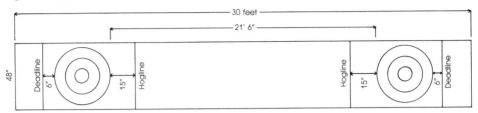

6. Games shall consist of 20 ends; change ends each half (10 ends).

7. Balls shall be delivered through the center ring and released at the dead line at the back of the center ring.

8. At the commencement of each end the Kitty (or Jack) is placed on the spot in center ring. When the ball has displaced the Kitty and is directly on the spot or near it, the Kitty shall be placed behind the ball and as close to the spot as possible without disturbing the ball or balls.

NOTE—The Rules outlined above are most widely used. There are no official rules and each club may adopt special house rules more suitable.

There are six players on each team and each player bowls two balls during the game. Since, as in shuffleboard, only half of each team bowls at any given time, (ie. three people from each team) a set of carpet bowls would consist of twelve balls (six pairs of balls) plus the jack, making a total of thirteen. These six pairs of balls have to be either differently colored or differently patterned so they can be distinguished when scoring. Commonly, the six bowls belonging to one team will be lined or striped and the six bowls belonging to the other team will be spotted. In fact, the Anglican Church league rules for 1949–1950 specified that stripes would lead in the first half and spots in the second half. To complete the unique identity of the pairs of bowls, colors were used. Three colors, often the same colors, were used for the bowls of each team. Thus two of the lined bowls would be green and two of the spotted bowls would be green, two lined bowls yellow and two spotted bowls yellow, two lined bowls red and two spotted bowls red, as an example.

Earlier rules from Thomas Taylor specified four players on a team rather than six. They also indicated that scoring depended upon the closeness of the bowls to the jack rather than on their position in any fixed target circle; in fact, circular targets were not even mentioned. In addition they gave the width of the carpet as being 6' while Margesson's rules indicated 4' and the Anglican Church rules for the 1940s indicated only 3'. If in the earlier version of the game scoring could be altered by hitting and moving the jack (ie. the jack would not be replaced if it was hit), then a carpet width of 6' would seem to be necessary, since this less controlled style of play would demand a larger playing area. Apparently as play became more restrictive by the addition of stationary target circles, the width of the carpet could be reduced; thus carpet width declined as the need to follow the jack around disappeared. The earlier free-style form with its multiple ways of changing the scoring (and the outcome of the game) must have been a very wild and wonderful affair to watch. But then what else would be expected of a bunch of Scots in the 1800s? In fact, the free-style game seems very much suited to 19th century Scots, and the target circle game very much suited to 20th century church-going Anglicans.

Collectible Carpet Bowls

Carpet bowls were certainly produced in Scotland, almost certainly in England, and possibly in Canada. An unknown variety of carpet bowl was also produced at Troy, Indiana in the 1840s (see china section, Chapter Two—Carskadden and Gartley, 1990 B). Thomas Taylor Bowls Limited has already been mentioned as a manufacturer in Glasgow, Scotland whose founding dated back to 1796. Potteries at Bo-ness on the River Forth were supposedly the most prolific producers of the early ceramic spheres (Biernacki, 1984). The same antiques dealer in Edinburgh that I mentioned earlier also told me that bowls had been produced on the Isle of Fife in the Firth (Bay) of Forth. I had to have him repeat this information about three times. If you wonder why, try saying, in the appropriate Scottish accent, "Ay laddie on the Isle of Fife in the Firth of Forth." Now try saying it at about the speed of light, which is the rate at which this gentleman tended to carry on a conversation.

The bowls usually have a brown ceramic inner body, which was subjected to a high firing to resist impact. The white glaze around the outside is probably tin oxide, fired at a slightly lower temperature than the core, but still at a higher temperature than the color. Color, usually in the form of some other oxide, was either painted on, applied with a sponge, or stamped with an applicator having a sponge-like texture. The latter would be dipped in the color or oxide and the bowl would be turned as the pattern was stamped on it in concentric circles. The bowl was then fired a third time at a low temperature to set the colors. Even mint carpet bowls often have three small holes in the glaze in roughly a triangular pattern. These represent the three points of a tripod on which the bowl was supported in the kiln while it was being fired. Carpet bowls come in a variety of sizes, but the standard size usually given is $3\frac{1}{4}''$ in diameter. However, bowls in my collection range from just over $2\frac{1}{2}''$ to just under $3\frac{1}{2}''$ in diameter, and smaller "child size" bowls can be found (Plates 6 and 7).

Since each carpet bowl set came with only one jack and twelve bowls, one would think that the jacks would be rarer and more collectible. However, since all of the jacks are plain white while bowls came in varied colors and patterns (even within a set), many of the unusual bowl patterns are far rarer than the jacks are, not to mention being more attractive. Jacks tended to vary in size but were usually about $2\frac{1}{2}''$ in diameter. Although jacks in general are not held in the same esteem that the bowls are, some jacks are quite rare, especially those bearing the names and locations of the companies that made the carpet bowl sets (Plate 6, lower right). Among names found on jacks are Taylor-Rolph, London; Harold, Wilson and Company, Toronto; A.G. Spalding, Great Britain; Jacques, London, and W. Sykes, London and Horbury.

Note the two versions of the Taylor-Rolph brand on Plate 6. Which do you think is older? One is in flowing script; the other is in print, and includes the words "Co. Limited" after the Taylor-Rolph name. I wish I could have pictured both sides of these, since Taylor-Rolph jacks have a trade-mark on the back. The trademark says "IMP brand" and pictures an elf (or imp) sitting on top of a circle with one leg bent and the other extended. Inside the circle is a hodge-podge of small symbols and tiny print. Below the circle on the print jack are the words "trade mark"; below the circle on the script jack are the words "trade mark," and below that "Made in England." Thus the script jack, which appears older to most people, was made after 1890, while the other was made at an earlier date.

As the rules for the game indicate, most carpet bowl patterns can be placed into one of two major groups, either lines or spots. By lined I mean a pattern of thin intersecting concentric circles which form a grid pattern in the middle of the bowl such as those on Plate 6 (center right). On almost all bowls the lines are of a single color. Occasionally one will see a bowl with two different colored lines such as the red and black, and green and black ones illustrated on Plate 7 (lower center and left). Such bowls are extremely rare. I enumerated by pattern both the carpet bowls in my father's collection and those in the much larger collection of John Moore, many of which were offered for sale between 1981 and 1985. These carpet bowls totaled 607, and of that number 287 or 47% were lined (Table 3-1). It is both amazing and reassuring that this number came out so close to 50%, since 50% is exactly what would be expected if one half of each carpet bowl set were lined bowls.

The sponged on (spot) designs offered more freedom of expression for the different companies making carpet bowls, thus there is more variation in these patterns than in the lined patterns. One design does however dominate the spot patterns; I refer to this pattern as dot-and-crown (Plate 6, cranberry pair, upper right). Dot and crown consists of a large solid colored dot surrounded by a white frilled area. This pattern comprises 31% of all the carpet bowls enumerated and 58% of all the non-lined carpet bowls. I suspect that this pattern was produced by a major company which made carpet bowls over a long period of time, but I don't know which company. A variety of similar patterns are much less common, comprising only 8% of the carpet bowls as a group (Table 3-1). On Plate 6, these include dot-and-star (lower 3, left row), doughnut-and-star (lower 2 of upper left 5), doughnut-and-crown (top 2 of upper left 5), open star (center of upper left 5), or dot-and-doughnut (center-right, top 2 rows). Any of these patterns just mentioned make up less than 2% of the total individually.

Another pattern making up 8% of the bowls counted is called banded cross (Plate 7, bottom and lower right). These have two broad bands which intersect each other in the center of the bowl, and finer parallel lines that add to the decoration. The broad bands are often a different color from the parallel lines, giving these bowls a particularly striking appearance. The bullseye, another strikingly attractive pattern, make up only 3% of the total bowls looked at. These bowls have several variations, including a combination of thin and broad concentric circles running from one end of the sphere to the other, a broad bullseye on each end with fine concentric circles in between, and solid circles or dots surrounded by thin, intersecting concentric circles (Plate 6, lower center and

TABLE 3-1   RELATIVE RARITY (%) OF CARPET BOWLS BY PATTERN (SAMPLE SIZE = 607)

Lined	Dot & Crown	Other "Spot"	Banded	Bullseye	Sponge & Spatter	Other
47%	31%	8%	8%	3%	1%	1%

Plate 7, lower center and center left). Again the fact that the broader bands are differently colored from some of the finer concentric circles gives these bowls a very attractive appearance.

Now we get to talk about those patterns that are extremely rare, including the spatter and sponge types (Table 3-1). Although all of the patterns were applied with a sponge of some type, those I referred to as "sponge" have random patterns of color without any discernable dots or stars (Plate 7, green and red pair, center right). The spatter pattern looks just like spatter-ware with dots of two colors (green and red) scattered at random around the surface of the bowl (Plate 7, center right). Both of these types are extremely rare. Another extremely rare bowl is one that looks like it has been sectioned like an orange. (Perhaps these should be called Orange Bowls.) Pairs of rings divide this bowl into even quarters (Plate 7, upper left). Another very rare type I refer to as "chain-link". The yellow example pictured shows how an open star base pattern was used to form a larger chain-link pattern around the bowl (Plate 7, upper row center). Other extremely rare types include those decorated with shamrocks, flowers, or even hearts, such as the blue shamrock shown (Plate 6, center left). Also seldom seen are bowls with any design having a mocha or tan rather than white base color (Plate 6, lower center). All of these types are extremely rare and the individual kinds make up only a fraction of a percent of the total looked at. It is a lucky individual who has an example or two of these in his collection.

Two final oddball specimens which fit into the general "carpet bowl" category are wooden spheres with designs formed by the heads of iron, brass, and copper nails pounded into them (Plate 7, top and upper right). The dealer I purchased these from said they were "French boules" which dated from 1850 to 1900. The one at the bottom of Plate 7 has the initials D and F on different segments, while the other has only the star pattern. I have no other information on these at present.

Flash warning! As this was going to press, I learned that carpet bowls were being reproduced and sold through advertisements in such magazines as *Country Living*. Unfortunately, these seem to be fairly good reproductions of a variety of the early patterns. They are being hand-made in Scotland (near Glasgow) and retailed (at about $65) through Colfax and Fowler in London and Lee Bogart (an importer) in the U.S. Those who have seen these reproductions say that they are distinguishable from the old ones. Get an ad or ask for a description of the new ones available so you can recognize them. Also (as said of other items) buy bowls with a known history.

₀4₀
History and Production of Cane Cut Glass Marbles

History of German Marbles

Exactly when and where the first glass sphere was produced to be used as a toy is something that we will probably never know. We have fair evidence that glass marbles date to Roman times, and that glass spheres which could have been used as marbles go back even farther (see Introduction and Plate 28A.) However the first records we have of the production of the swirl and sulphide marbles collected today place the makers in the province of Thuringen, one of the toy making centers of Germany in the 1800s. Thuringen was in the East German zone at the time this chapter was written. Now, with reunification, we will be able to travel freely in Thuringen and obtain a more complete history of the old hand-cut glass marble industry.

Correspondence from the Museum for Glass Art states that the first glass marbles were made in the town of Lausche. Glass cottages (small factories which made glass items) began producing these marbles after a glassworker in Lausche invented a new tool, the "marbelschere" or marble scissors, in 1846. By rounding the marble completely in just one step, flawless and rapid production of marbles was possible. This tool enabled marbles to be produced in quantity for sale to the public. At that time, the glassworks already produced large quantities of "multicolored spun glass rods" (latticinio canes) for other products, and these became the favorite material for glass marbles. The demand for glass swirls became so great that in 1852 the son of glass master Elias Greiner's cousin received permission to build a new glassworks principally for the production of glass marbles. Marbles were produced at this same glass factory at least into the 1960s, although partially automated machines have been used since about 1926.

In my first edition, I suggested that marbles produced by twisting them off of glass canes piece by piece were made until about the end of World War I. This made sense at the time since the first World War would have interrupted the import trade, and since fairly modern machines capable of mass producing glass marbles were being perfected during this same period. However as the 1926 date for the beginning of automation indicates, the end of World War I is too early to mark the end of the handmade marble trade. The Sears Roebuck and Company catalog lists "Imported Glass (similar to the glass marbles sold before the war, with bright colored streamers through the center)" in its 1921 to 1923 editions (Randall and Webb, 1988). Furthermore, the Butler Brothers catalog of 1927 lists fine glass marbles and has an illustration of hand-cut swirls. Of course, illustrations might not really represent the marbles being sold. However, conclusive proof that old hand-cut swirl marbles were available for import comes from Germany itself.

Between about 1920 and 1930 the German toy industry tried to promote their export trade by printing a universal toy catalog, der Universal Spielwaren Katalog. The 1924–1926 editions of this catalog, taken from the toy museum located in Sonneberg, Thuringen, have been translated into English and Spanish and published with a commentary by Dr. Manfred Bachmann. The universal toy catalog combines the export offerings of almost the entire German toy industry at the time. On page 357 of this catalog are pictured a series of latticinio core swirl marbles with two and three color ribbons for outer decoration. These marbles were obviously produced by hand cutting from a cane. Ten different sizes are listed as being available and seven of these are shown in a long triangular box in which a series of marbles of increasing diameter would comfortably fit. Although the combined publication does not specify in which of the catalogs the marbles were shown, or if they were shown in both, we know for certain that such marbles were available for import at least in 1924 and probably in 1926. This checks with the information from the Museum for Glass Art that the Lausche glassworks produced marbles through the 1920s and beyond, and that machines were first used there about 1926. The illustration of hand-cut swirls that appears in the 1927 Butler Brothers catalog probably accurately records the type of marbles they had for sale, although those marbles may have represented a final sale of inventory produced and purchased a year or two earlier. This, combined with earlier dates for machine produced marbles (as we will discuss in Chapter 7) means that hand-cut and machine-made marbles competed with one another directly in the retail market for a period of at least 20 years.

How could such a situation exist for so long? How could handmade marbles produced with a great deal of labor compete successfully with machine-made marbles, especially when the former had to be imported? What made this possible were the conditions in Germany following World War I. During World War I much of the toy industry in Germany was re-geared to make parts for military uniforms or other articles that could be used during the war. After the war, workers returned to their original products and tried to regain their former market. However, workers in the toy industry in general, and especially in the small home industries (like the sulphide marble makers), were put under severe stress by the devaluation of the German mark which occurred between 1918 and 1923.

The following description of conditions in 1923 is given by Manfred Bachmann and attributed to him by Stephen Zweig. "In the history of mankind currency never and nowhere recorded such staggering fits and starts as in 1923 in Germany. As prices rose feverishly, a shoelace all of a sudden cost more than had a shoe a few days earlier, and was even more expensive than thousands of pairs of luxury footwear a week previously. Beggars became multimillionaires yet re-mained hungry . . . . Workers heaved their weekly earnings, which had formerly fitted into a narrow packet, back home in rucksacks, laundry baskets and, if they didn't spend everything at once, were hardly able to pay for as much coal as the bank notes weighed. Indeed, prices often doubled within hours. The amount needed in the morning for a pound of meat would hardly suffice for a crust in the evening. Savings which official's wives had put aside assiduously for decades would now barely do for a tramway ticket. The bank note presses, unremittedly fed by three hundred paper works operating to full capacity, delivered million and billion denomination bills day and night which, hardly had the ink dried, were again valueless and could only be retained as a short term currency by overprints with still more naughts."

Foreign capital, particularly American concerns, eagerly exploited the infla-tion in Germany. The situation in Sonneberg, the principle toy center in

Thuringen, was typical of what was happening in Germany as a whole. U.S. firms would either buy out German toy industries or set up "buying branches" to purchase toys from all the German makers. In 1913 Woolworth started a buying branch in Sonneberg to handle purchases solely for New York. This company established direct links with small and very small producers of toys. Exports ran at 10 to 11 million marks per year over ten years. Between 8 hundred and 9 hundred companies supplied toys to Woolworth of which 25% were independent home based workers. Often these small manufacturers would be given materials to compensate for the lack of wages. In 1925 Woolworth gathered in almost 25 million dollars. Other American firms which established buying outlets in Sonneberg included Kresge, Kress, Burgfledt, Butler Brothers, Lewis Wolf and others. Speculative buying out of German industries reached its greatest point in 1922 and 1923 because of the constantly declining German mark, which, at the end of this period, was so worthless that one dollar was equivalent to 4.2 billion marks.

The falling mark and foreign monopolies kept many German workers impoverished. Again this was especially true of small cottage factories and home workers. Quoting again from Manfred Bachmann, "The most terrible forms of children's labor are prevalent virtually without exception in the toy industry. Even the smallest, not yet of school age, worked day-in day-out making articles intended to give children pleasure. They have become a scourge for those engaged in their manufacture. Indeed frequently enough despite the assistance of the children, hourly rates are a mere 7 to 12 pfennigs, for instance for the manufacture of primitive metal toys in the Nurenberg area. The result is that the working day extends well into the night."

Since a pfennig is one one-hundredth of a mark and billions of marks were needed to equal the value of a dollar, it is no wonder that the German handmade marbles could compete in price with those manufactured in the United States. It was only because they were being paid virtually nothing that the German glass workers could compete with the churning machines of Peltier, Akro Agate, and others. This gives a bittersweet edge to those marbles produced during the last years of hand manufacture. The same marbles which were played with in the sunshine by happy children in the U.S. may have been produced, at least in part, by the labor of hungry children working at night in Germany.

Child labor, of course, was quite common in the 1800s and "family" businesses, such as marble making, would have used children in the glass factories. The following is an excerpt from Roberts' (1883) article, "Marbles and Where They Come From."

All the dealers in marbles—and I have talked with very many of them—tell me that the entire stock of marbles for the American market comes from Germany, and that the prices paid for manufacturing them are so low that no American laborer would or could live on such wages. A great deal of the work, such as moulding and painting, is performed by poor little children.

"I shall never again watch a lot of happy, intelligent, bright, well-fed, and well-clothed American boys playing at marbles but I shall think of the poorly clad German children munching away on a piece of black bread (for that is all they get to eat) as they work on their weary tasks for a few cents a week. Poor little things! It is no wonder they love America, and wish they were human marbles and could roll over here.

A few American companies may also have produced handmade marbles. Certainly a few handmade marbles were produced at factories engaged in the production of other types of glass items, or even in early factories producing machine-made marbles. Such marbles were made by workers in their spare time either as a treat for their children or as a demonstration of their skill. Very few American companies produced handmade glass marbles as a production item. One factory that did reportedly do this (Righter, 1982) was the Iowa City Flint Glass Manufacturing Company founded on April 30, 1880 by J.H. Leighton. The factory was only in operation for 15 or 20 months and failed in 1882. However, during their brief period of business they did manufacture marbles, one of which is in the possession of the Iowa City Historical Museum. The marble is described as having a diameter of about $1\frac{1}{2}$ times that of a silver dollar. Four swirling bands which are alternately red and white and green and white give the marble its color. Other clear marbles of various sizes with spiraled threads of color have also been authenticated as products of the Iowa City Factory, and sulphides with figures of animals and birds are said to have been made there, although this has never been verified.

Certainly sulphides depicting American presidents or American coins (there are sulphides depicting both an 1858 seated Liberty quarter and an Indian head penny) would probably have been produced at a U.S. factory. Mr. Leighton was involved in other glass companies before and after the Iowa City factory, particularly in and around the city of Akron, Ohio in the 1890s and early 1900s, and it is known that at least some of these companies also produced marbles. However, no known marbles (at this time) can be attributed to Leighton except those at Iowa City (cane cut swirls) and those at Navarre (see transition marbles, Chapter Seven). It is not clear when he made the switch from cane cut to the new gathering process needed for transition marbles. Hopefully, collectors will refrain from calling cane cut opaques "Leighton marbles" unless it is documented that he produced these.

Another factory mentioned in my first edition as probably having produced handmade marbles was the Boston and Sandwich Glass Company in Massachusetts. However a number of books whose authors have done extensive research on the Boston and Sandwich Glass Company fail to mention glass marbles as a production item. This includes a book whose focus was witch balls, containers and toys (Barlow and Kaiser, 1987). Therefore although Boston and Sandwich glass workers may have made marbles for their children, there seems to be no hard evidence that marbles were ever a production item at the factory. More will be said about the Boston and Sandwich Glass Factory in Chapter 5. The Navarre Glass Marble and Specialty Company of Navarre, Ohio was also mentioned in my first edition as producing hand-cut marbles. This company will be discussed in detail in the Transition Marble section in Chapter 7. Suffice it to say here that hand-cut swirl and sulphide marbles were not production items at this factory.

The first step in the production of hand-cut glass marbles was the production of the glass cane. In order to make these rods, a glass worker would take a blow pipe and roll a glass mass approximately 6″ long on its end (Miller, 1966). Next hot glass rods of various colors were placed in the grooves of an iron sheet which was also 6″ long. The glass bar was then carefully rolled over the sheet allowing the colored rods in the grooves to attach themselves, one after another, to the larger bar. If the rods were placed in consecutive grooves on the sheet they would be adjacent to one another on the rod and a solid column would result in the marble. If the rods were separated from each other by one or two grooves, an open swirl effect would be produced. The bar was then covered with clear glass by the glass worker. If another ring of colored rods was desired in the marble, the process was repeated. Finally the bar was pulled and twisted to a diameter of $1\frac{1}{2}$″ to $2\frac{1}{2}$″ and to a length of approximately $6\frac{1}{2}$′. Eight to twelve of these bars would then be stored, ready for use, in an oven. Before these rods were formed into marbles they might be reheated, pulled, and twisted to make marbles of smaller diameter, or they might be used as they were for larger marbles.

Marbles were cut off the glass rods by the marble scissors (Fig. 4-1). These scissors were hand-smithed and consisted of a flexible strip of iron formed into the shape of a "U" and resembling a pair of tongs. On the right hand end was a round bottom cup or "marble mold" and on the left was a knife-like blade. As the drawing indicates the marble bowl or cup was attached only with a screw. This allowed cups of different sizes to be interchanged with each other on the same scissors. Light pressure in the middle of the scissors caused the two ends to come together, the lip of the cup forming the other half of the scissors with the blade.

For the forming process the hot end of the glass cane would be pressed into the cup and turned several times with enough pressure to round it. Then the two ends of the scissors were pressed together and the tool was twisted slowly around until the blade had completely separated the soft piece of glass from the glass cane. After the marbles hardened slightly they were placed in a cylindrical wooden barrel. The marble maker kept this barrel continually rotating with one foot while the glass spheres gradually cooled off and became round. For the final cooling the marbles were picked up with an iron spoon and placed in an annealing (slow cooling) oven in lots of 10 to 20. Several marbles would be cut from the cane at one time until the glass bar had cooled to the point where it required reheating. Several different methods were used to polish the marbles. Most marbles either had a natural fire polish, or could be reheated until the glass became soft again. An acid polish could also be produced by dipping the marbles into an acid solution. Finally a dull polish could be obtained by tumbling the marbles in a large rotating metal drum which contained a mixture of water and a polishing compound.

The Making of a Marble

In order to get more insight into how the old glass marbles were produced, I decided to interview a modern glass artist who specializes in marbles and watch his production technique. I chose Mark Matthews, an independent glass artist in residence at the Sauder Farm and Craft Village located in Ohio, who produces marbles in the old style as well as contemporary looking marbles. He decided that a German swirl type of marble with a lobed or ridged core and a series of fifteen outer swirls representing the different colors of the visable spectrum would capture the old German flavor but have a contemporary flair. The core itself was to be a tan color with dark umber accents on the edge of the ridges (more German flavor). Since my limited information from Germany gave no clue as to how lobed or ridged core marbles were formed, I felt that watching Mark produce these marbles could be a very educational experience.

First Mark demonstrated how a single colored glass cane could be formed.

Fig. 4-1. Marble cutting scissors.

Fig. 4-2. A hot cylinder of clear glass is rolled in colored powdered glass.

Fig. 4-3. The heated glass is brought to the marver and pressed down to form a long rectangle.

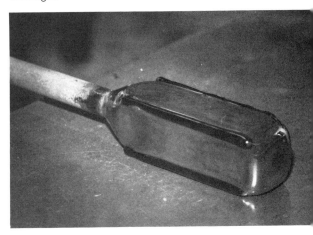

Fig. 4-4. A marble is cut from the end of the stock.

Fig. 4-5. A glass cane is rolled over colored rods to create a swirl marble.

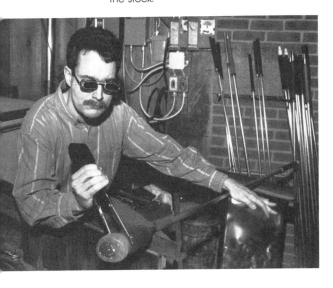

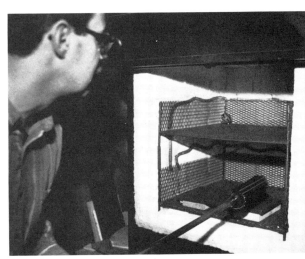

Fig. 4-6. The marver is used to taper the marble on one end.

Fig. 4-7. A graphite tool is used to size and shape the marble.

Once formed, such canes could be broken into short segments and used to decorate cores or to form outer spirals in swirl marbles. The tip of a punty rod, a long hollow metal rod with about a 6″ solid tip, was heated to a red/orange glow. It was then used to stick or pick up a chunk of 1000°F cadmium yellow glass from the annealing oven. Glass at 1000°F is still stiff as a brick; it must be heated in the furnace at about 2300°F to make it workable. When the glass became soft enough it was taken out of the furnace and rolled on a marver, basically a table top of steel or marble, to shape the glass into a short thick cylinder. This solid cylinder was then fire polished, dipped into molten clear glass in the tank within the furnace, and then rolled again to form a slightly larger cylinder with a thin layer of clear over the yellow glass. This outer clear layer shields the inner colored glass from the direct fire. Once this two-layered cylinder was the proper temperature, Mark carried it, still on the tip of his punty rod, to a spot with plenty of open space.

Mark's wife Ruth then grabbed the end of the glass with a pair of diamond shears and began to pull gently. At a slow steady pace Ruth backed up, pulling the rod which became longer and longer and narrower and narrower. They then held the rod in the air until it cooled sufficiently to be placed on the floor without cracking from the temperature change. It amazed me that even at relatively high temperatures, a long, very narrow rod would remain straight instead of bowing or bending in the middle.

Mark then proceeded to start making the marbles. First he took a rainbow assortment of glass canes and placed them in the pasterelli, a metal plate with evenly spaced grooves for holding canes in a predetermined arrangement. The pasterelli was then placed into the 1000°F annealing oven. For the core of the marble, Mark first gathered clear glass from the furnace and again shaped it into a short rod or cylinder on the metal marver. This procedure was repeated until enough clear had been gathered to form the correct core size. This hot cylinder of clear glass was then rolled in a powdered tan glass (Fig. 4-2), placed back into the furnace and reheated, rolled on the marver to regain its shape, and rolled again in tan powder. This procedure of coating the core with tan glass and reheating it was repeated about 15 times. I had always assumed that the thin base color in solid core antique swirls or the base color of white or yellow found on onionskins had been applied by dipping the clear glass center into liquid yellow or white glass. However the old makers probably also rolled these cores in powdered glass of the appropriate color. Mark heated the glass once more, brought it to the marver, and pressed down on the cylinder first one side and then the other to form a long rectangle with a square cross section. Next he carefully picked up the four thick umber canes from the annealing oven with the hot glass rectangle, placing one cane on each edge. The rectangle with the umber rods was then heated and squared twice more until the canes fused into the edges (Fig. 4-3).

At this point, a casing of clear glass could be added over the core. Having the right temperature was crucial. The core needed to be cool enough that the color didn't run or bleed into the new hot glass, but not so cold that blisters or bubbles would form between the colored glass and the clear. At the right moment Mark put the colored glass core into the furnace and submerged it into the clear molten glass within. He pulled out this new heavier mass of glass and once again rolled it on the marver shaping it into a cylinder. Inside the clear glass cylinder lay the square core with the umber rods on its edges. It was cased again to attain the proper spacing between the core and the still-to-be-added outer swirls. Now came a part of the process which differs from the old way of doing things. Instead of keeping the assembly straight, Mark put a "pre-twist" on the core. He did this by angling the gathering rod and putting pressure just on the tip of the glass cylinder as he rolled it on the marver. As the cylinder of glass was rolled along the marver the pressure on the tip caused the glass within to twist. There, before your eyes, you could see what used to be a square center turning into a lobed or ridged core center. The twisting had the effect of bringing the edges of the square out as ridges and the centers of the square in as valleys. Once again Mark worked with the furnace and the marver to get the cylinder of glass to the correct diameter. At this point Mark cut a marble from the end of the stock (Fig. 4-4), partly to reduce the stock to the correct mass. This marble, a larger size than that selected for the final product, clearly shows the core detail (Plate 18A upper right).

Now Mark went back to the annealing oven to pick up the fifteen solid colored glass canes that would make up the outer rainbow swirls. Since these swirls are meant to be close to each other on the marble, the rods have been laid in adjacent grooves of the iron pasterelli. This means that Mark must be extremely careful in keeping his glass cylinder straight while rolling it over the glass canes (Fig. 4-5). If he angled the glass cylinder at some point, he'd have canes crisscrossing each other or angling towards one another. After the colored canes were picked up, they were rolled on the marble marver, reheated and rolled again. This process is repeated to "marver the canes into the surface." However just the right touch had to be used since the canes couldn't be allowed to flatten out, or they would make the central core difficult to view. A final casing of clear was added over the entire construction and, after shaping, another twist was applied again using pressure at the tip of the cylinder of glass on the steel marver.

The marble stock was never pulled into a cane as was the fashion in the old days. Instead it was reheated in the furnace and then tapered on the end using the marble marver (Fig. 4-6). When the glass reached the right temperature a graphite tool with a circular depression was used to help size and shape the marble (Fig. 4-7). Cutting the marble from the rod was accomplished with a variety of instruments, including an oversized pair of tweezers (jacks) (see Fig. 4-4) and an ancient dinner knife. When only a small thread of glass holds the marble to the rest of the marble stock, the marble is placed onto a hemispherical depression in a refractory brick, and the gathering rod is gently tapped, breaking the thin glass thread and dropping the marble into its little nest. The top of the marble is then heated with a torch, excess glass is pulled and sheared from the surface, and the remainder is rounded into the top of the marble.

Each of the marbles had a perfectly fire-polished surface, and no further finishing was necessary. After the tops of the marbles were finished each marble was taken from the brick and placed carefully in the annealing oven. The annealing process for the $1\frac{1}{4}''$ marbles being produced took 12 hours, after which the colorful spheres were finally finished (Plate 18B, lower right). If the glass cooled too quickly it could become unstable and break at anytime. The length of the annealing process was determined by the thickness of the piece of glass being cooled.

While Mark was finishing the marble, Ruth took the marble stock and placed it back into the furnace to keep it hot. If it's not kept above 1000°F, uncontrolled cooling would cause it to crack apart. Ruth also twists and shears the top of the marble stock to bring the swirls to a perfect point just in time to hand it over to Mark to begin the marble cutting process again. The tapering and cutting procedure was repeated over and over as one marble after another was painstakingly cut from the end of the marble stock. One of the things that you learn from watching Mark and talking with him is that a variety of different procedures can produce the same effect in a glass marble. Thus we may not know the techniques used by the old German masters until we are able to rummage around in Germany and see what old records we can turn up.

$\circ 5 \circ$
Cane Cut Glass Marbles

German Swirls

German swirls or spirals are the most common of the old glass marbles cut from canes. These marbles were called German spirals or candy-stripes in my old edition, but the term German swirls seems to be more commonly used today. German swirls include all those marbles cut from glass canes except for onion-skins, opaque marbles, and micas. Even colored glass marbles and lutz marbles are simply variations of the German swirl. However the term is usually used to refer to marbles of clear glass which have either a latticinio core, a solid core, a divided core, or a ribbon center. Also included in this group would be marbles of clear glass which have bands or lines of decoration towards the outside of the marble but have no real core.

Of the three main core types found in German swirls, latticinio centers (or net centers) are the most common (Plates 8 and 9), occurring in about 62% of all the smaller marbles. Solid cores (Plates 10 and 11) and divided cores (Plates 12 and 13) are about equally common with each occurring around 20% of the time in smaller marbles (Table 5-1). Note that in the smaller size groups, $\frac{5}{8}''$ and $\frac{3}{4}''$ marbles, are by far the most common (Table 5-1). Of marbles ranging between $\frac{1}{2}''$ and $1''$ in size only 4% are smaller than $\frac{5}{8}''$. While collectors have always paid a

TABLE 5-1   RELATIVE RARITY OF SIZES AND CORE TYPES OF GERMAN SWIRLS

Dia.	Latticinio	Solid	Divided	Total	% of G.T.
$\frac{1}{2}''$	25	2	7	34	4%
$\frac{5}{8}''$	250	54	66	370	46%
$\frac{3}{4}''$	189	66	52	307	38%
$\frac{7}{8}''$	31	17	28	76	9%
$1''$	6	5	6	17	2%
Total	**501**	**144**	**159**	**804**	
% of Grand Total	**62%**	**18%**	**20%**		

premium for larger marbles, it seems appropriate to also pay a premium for the smallest of the marbles, those which were smaller than the normal playing size. Certainly they are far less common than those of $\frac{5}{8}''$ to $\frac{3}{4}''$ which were commonly used in the various marble games.

Incidently, data in Table 5-1 and other tables comes largely from my collection and my father's and, in some cases, is combined with data taken from surveys at major marble shows, such as the Amana Show or the Columbus Show. The broad base of my collection was acquired more or less at random. That is, I didn't specialize in any particular type of marble. However in my collection, and certainly in the marbles on display at the major marble shows, there will be a bias towards rarer types. While I or another advanced collector might pass up a marble of a common type, we certainly would not pass up an opportunity to buy a rare or unusual marble. Thus whatever is shown in these tables to be scarce is likely to be even rarer yet were a truly unbiased survey done.

This table, and the others in this book, are provided to give you an idea of what is common and what is not. Minor differences of percentages in these tables, for instance the difference between 18% and 20% for solid and divided cores in Table 5-1, probably are not meaningful. Thus Table 5-1 demonstrates a real difference in the rarity of latticinio core marbles as opposed to solid and divided core, but does not, in my opinion, show any real difference in the rarity of solid core and divided core marbles. Similarly data on the same table shows a real difference between the rarity of $\frac{5}{8}''$ and $\frac{3}{4}''$ marbles and that of $\frac{1}{2}''$ or $\frac{7}{8}''$ marbles. However it does not demonstrate much difference between the rarity of $\frac{5}{8}''$ marbles and $\frac{3}{4}''$ marbles. Remember too that the larger the sample size (N) or number of marbles looked at, the more accurate the percentages given will be. Thus a table based on 500 marbles will be more trustworthy (especially for smaller differences) than a table based on 50 marbles.

Latticinio Core

Latticinio or net cores are the most common of the old cane cut antique marbles. The reason that they are so common is because they enjoyed a long and popular sales history, due no doubt to their natural attractiveness. They were apparently among the very last marbles to have been fashioned by hand from canes, since they appear in the Universal German Toy Catalog of 1924 to 1926. Interestingly neither the other core types nor sulphides appear in that magazine. They were probably also among the first marbles produced with the new marble scissors, although the earliest dated examples we have for cane-cut marbles are onionskins, micas, and open-core German swirls. Certainly a great deal of skill was required to pull and twist the glass rods to the point where previously thick, parallel rods of white glass became thin, white threads of glass twisting around a clear center core to give the illusion of forming a net. However canes of this type had been made at the glass cottages prior to the production of marbles. These marbles did, however, require some outer decoration. Thus a glassworker making such a marble would have to do two levels of work; he would have to take clear glass, roll it over the rods which would make the latticinio core, add more clear glass, roll it over more rods to make the outer coloration, then perhaps add even more clear glass. In a few marbles of the latticinio type and of the solid and divided core types, three levels of decoration are present. Because such workmanship was at a premium, these marbles are extremely rare.

In my first edition, I divided the latticinio cores according to the types of outer decoration on the marble. I have since decided that the core pattern and coloration is more important than the outer decoration. Thus in this book I will emphasize the types and colors of the latticinio core itself. However please note that some of these marbles have different patterns of outer decoration than others. Even though I won't discuss these differences in this book, owners of my old book or price guide will note that I valued some of the types of outer decoration higher than others. Remember that it is the characteristics of marbles not mentioned in books which give the sharp collector a buying advantage.

Latticinio cores come primarily in white and yellow, but a few contain oranges and reds. I have not seen any other colors in a typical, tightly spun latticinio core. White cores predominate; making up over 60% of the marbles in both large and small sizes (Table 5-2, Plate 8, upper portion). Yellow cores are also relatively common making up about 24% of both large and small marbles (Plate 8, lower portion), although this makes them only $\frac{1}{3}$ as abundant as the white cores. Orange and red cores occur slightly more often in small marbles, those of 1″ or less, than in large marbles. Marbles larger than 1″ with an orange latticinio core are extremely rare. I have never seen a large marble in which the actual threads of the latticinio core were red; the 1% mentioned in Table 5-2 and pictured in Plate 9 (upper center) consists of a single marble in which the actual threads are white, but are surrounded by an envelope of translucent red glass. However in smaller marbles actual red and red-orange threads are sometimes used (see Collecting Small Swirls in this chapter and Plate 24). Conversely, alternating white and yellow threads or alternating groups of white and yellow threads are more common in large marbles than they are in small marbles (Table 5-2). In fact, alternating groups of white and yellow, the rarer of the two types, was not found in the 454 small marbles examined. I have only seen one marble in which definitely orange colored threads alternated with white in the core (Plate 28E, left) and one in which orange alternated with yellow (Plate 28E, right); both color combinations produce a striking effect.

A seldom seen variation on the latticinio center is one which includes broader bands of color as an integral part of the latticinio core. I only own three examples of these "banded latticinios," which should give you some idea of their rarity. These three range from 1 $\frac{7}{8}$″ to 2 $\frac{1}{4}$″ in diameter. The largest has three red bands each with a yellow stripe down the center, subdividing the white threads in

TABLE 5-2   RELATIVE RARITY (%) OF LATTICINIO CORE COLORS

Marble Size	Sample Size	White	Yellow	Orange	Red	Alt. White & Yellow	Grouped White & Yellow
Small (≤1″)	454	61%	24%	9%	2%	4%	0%
Large (≥1$\frac{1}{8}$″)	106	62%	24%	2%	1%*	8%	3%

* White lines surrounded by translucent red envelope.

the latticinio core into three segments. The other two alternate groups of yellow and white threads, separating these groups with colored bands. In the most striking of these, opposing pairs of translucent green and opaque red and translucent blue and opaque red separate two groups of three yellow and two groups of three white threads in the core. An outer decoration of evenly spaced opaque red bands complete a well-designed and well-crafted marble (Plate 28D, right).

Another rare type of marble is the latticinio ribbon. These marbles have two bands each consisting of parallel threads of glass with the bands themselves set parallel and close to each other. The threads in each band are angled in opposite directions, thus achieving the crossing or latticinio effect in the form of a ribbon rather than a column-like core. I have only seen four of these, three of which were large (about 1 3/4" to 2"). In the first, both halves of the ribbon consist of yellow threads and the edges of the ribbon are bordered by red bands (Plate 28D, center). The second had white threads in one half of the ribbon and yellow in the other, giving a white and yellow crossing pattern to the latticinio (Plate 28D, left). The third had alternating white and yellow threads in each half of the ribbon, with the ends again bordered by red bands. The single small marble has yellow threads in both halves of the ribbon, and both halves are bordered with blue bands. The banding would imply that the first and third and small marbles were by the same maker. Large latticinio ribbons have a rarity comparable to that of large clambroths.

The twelve latticinio marbles pictured in Plate 8 are evenly split between white core and yellow core examples. These range in size from 2 3/8" in diameter for the large yellow core at the bottom to 1 1/4" in diameter for the smaller orangish core in the lower center. Notice that the yellow color in the latticinio centers does run the gamut from a light yellow to an orange. Other things to notice on the plate include the variation in the amount of twist put into the latticinio center, both in terms of the individual threads and of the core itself; the large white latticinio core marble with the red and blue outer decoration (center left) has a core which itself bows off to one side like a cyclone; and the differences in outer decoration on these marbles. Even two marbles which at a glance seem similar, such as the two large yellow latticinio cores at the bottom and right center of Plate 8 are in reality quite different. The one at the bottom has four bands of color, two bands of red on white alternating with one green on white and one blue on white, while the one right of center has six bands of color, three red on white alternating with three blue on white.

The latticinio cores on Plate 9 all fall into the rare category. The two marbles at the upper left and top of the plate have groups of yellow threads alternating with groups of white threads in the latticinio center. The latter is even rarer than those marbles in the lower portion of the plate, which have singly alternating white and yellow threads. The largest of these at bottom right measures $2\frac{1}{2}''$ in diameter, as does the white latticinio core marble at center right. The latter is included on the plate because it shows a segmented core with deliberate open spaces and tri-level workmanship. By this I mean that the white latticinio core is underneath the broad red stripes (which are really translucent red over white), which are themselves well underneath the outer pairs of thin blue lines. Thus the glassworker had to go through three separate processes of adding color and then adding further clear glass. Such tri-level marbles (as has been mentioned before) contain more workmanship than others and are, as would be expected, much rarer and more valuable than the normal two level marbles. The extremely rare marble with the red translucent envelope around a white latticinio core in the upper center of Plate 9 actually displays four levels of workmanship; (1) the white latticinio core, (2) the red envelope of translucent glass, (3) the two broad red and white bands alternating with blue and white and green and white bands, and (4) the thin pairs of yellow threads. All of these are at different levels within the glass. A marble with this much workmanship is, of course, extremely uncommon. This particular example measures $2\frac{1}{8}''$ in diameter.

Solid Core

A few solid core marbles (roughly 8%) look as though the core was produced by individual rods or ribbons of color. In other words it appears as though the glass master laid a long series of consecutive colored rods in the grooved iron tray, rolled the clear glass core over it until the entire core was covered with these rods, and then encased this in further clear glass. This would produce a solid core composed of individual colored rods. However most solid cores appear to have been made by establishing a base color of white or yellow (or rarely blue, green, or red) and then applying other colored rods on top of that. While we are not sure how the old glassworkers did this, it is likely they used the same technique as Mark Matthews, rolling the clear base in powdered glass of white or yellow and reheating the mass. If this was then rolled over the groups of red, blue, and green rods spaced along the grooved iron sheet it would create the barber pole-like designs seen in many of the solid core marbles. While an opaque white glass was readily available, as can be seen in the clambroth type of marbles, most of the reds available to the old makers appear to have been fairly translucent. Therefore the only red core marbles that I have seen have the red backed by a layer of white. Solid core marbles also come in both ridged and non-ridged styles. While the lobes in most lobed-onionskins are gently rounded like hills, the ridges in solid core marbles often come to a sharp or even knife-like edge. Thus I prefer to call these ridged because of the sharpness of the edge, rather than lobed.

The two most important characteristics in determining the value of solid core marbles are the style of the core (whether it is ridged or not) and the base color of the core. Ridged marbles (Plate 10, bottom) make up almost one quarter of all the larger solid cores but are very rare in small marbles (Table 5-3). Ridged cores with a yellow base (Plate 10, lower left) are also very rare. I have only seen two marbles in which white and yellow base colors alternate in a ridged core. One of these was decorated with red both on the ridges and in the valleys. The other had red on the ridges, but blue in the white valleys and green in the yellow valleys.

By far the most common solid core marbles are those which have a non-ridged or column core with a white base color (Plate 10, upper $\frac{2}{3}$); these make up over three quarters of both large and small solid core marbles. Column core marbles having a yellow base color are rare in small and very rare in large marbles, being only 5% of the total. Other colors such as blue, green, and red (Plate 11) were very seldom used as the base color for column core marbles, and I have never seen a ridged core marble in one of these colors. These different base colors combined comprise 5% or less of all the solid core marbles in either the small or large sizes (Table 5-3). In fact, it is interesting to note that even if one groups the blue, green, and red base colors together, they are at least as rare as the yellow based ridged marbles in the large sizes, and are much rarer than the white based

TABLE 5-3   RELATIVE RARITY (%) OF SOLID CORE TYPES AND COLORS

Marble Size	Sample Size	Ridged		Non-Ridged				
		White	Yellow	White	Yellow	Blue	Green	Red
Small (≤1″)	201	2%	0.5%	82%	11%	2%	1.5%	1%
Large (≥1⅛″)	62	18%	6%	76%	5%	3%	2%	0%

ridged marbles. Ask yourself how many solid cores you have seen with a red or green or blue base at any of the marble shows, and then compare that to the number of Lutz marbles you have seen of an equivalent size.

It is worthwhile to look at sub-categories of the white-based column core marbles, since they are the most numerous variety of solid core marble. In both large and small size groups, a large percentage (around one quarter) are made up of marbles decorated with red and blue, and an even larger percentage (30% to 40%) are marbles decorated with red, green, and blue (Table 5-4). The large marble group differs from the smaller marble group by having none (at least in those I surveyed) in which the white core is left undecorated, while 15% of the small marbles appear that way. Apparently a plain white core was thought to be dull and unattractive for a large marble. Similarly, more small marbles are decorated with a single color, most often red. Again this may have been considered simple or unattractive for a large marble. Other color combinations are unusual in both size categories, such as just blue (about 2% of both small and large marbles) and blue and green, which was about 4% of the small marbles and didn't appear in my sample of large marbles. With solid cores as with most marbles, rarity is often determined by whether or not the marble was appealing and could sell well, or by whether the additional labor needed added to its sales appeal. For instance, green and blue may have been too dark a color combination to make a good selling marble, and thus they were produced in low numbers. Also adding yellow to red, green, and blue may not have enhanced the marble enough to make the extra labor, or the expense of the extra colored rods, worth the increase in sales value.

A variety of the column and ridged core types which can be encountered is shown on Plate 10. The rarity of some of these such as the huge (2 $\frac{3}{8}$ +" in diameter) yellow ridged marble (lower left), the single color red on white (2 $\frac{1}{4}$" in

TABLE 5-4   RELATIVE RARITY (%) OF COLORS APPLIED TO WHITE-BASED SOLID CORES

Marble Size	Sample Size	None (White)	Single R	Double R&B	R&G	R,G,B	R,G,B,Y	Other
Small (≤1")	164	15%	9%	23%	9%	29%	5%	10%
Large (≥1⅛")	40	0	2.5	25%	5%	40%	12.5%	15%

R = red, B = blue, G = green, Y = yellow.

diameter, top center), and the yellow based marble (second from the top at right) have already been discussed. Note the differences in the white ridged marbles at center bottom and lower right. The one at center bottom has red ridges and blue valleys while the one at lower right has blue ridges and red valleys. In addition the one at center bottom has evenly spaced outer lines of yellow while the one at lower right has three groups of five yellow lines each. The large (2 $\frac{1}{4}''$ in diameter) marble at upper left is unusual in the use of a translucent red glass between bands of blue and green. Blues and greens were done in pairs or triplets giving the marble a somewhat segmented appearance, and the translucent red used over the opaque white gives the illusion of a pink core.

Other types of segmentation can be seen in the two center marbles. The upper marble has tight red, green, and blue bands formed by two or three adjacent rods each. The lower marble is mildly ridged and has segments of red and white alternating with segments of blue and white and green and yellow. The marble second from the top at the left has the traditional "barber pole" pattern with alternating single bands of red, green, and blue. The large marble at center right has green, yellow, red, and blue bands over the white. These bands are clearly spaced above the white with clear glass in between making it a three level production. Also on this marble we can clearly see that the white core was made from a series of adjacent white rods or ribbons. Thus several techniques were probably used in the production of the solid cores in these marbles.

Solid core marbles having a base color other than white are extremely rare as are all the examples in Plate 11. The large dark green and dark blue cores in the center right and lower right portion of Plate 11 are both over 2 $\frac{1}{8}''$ in diameter and, in my opinion, would be at least as rare as sulphide figures in colored glass and perhaps as rare as colored figures in sulphide marbles. The large blue core just mentioned also shows the three levels of workmanship mentioned previously as adding to the value of any marble. In this case we have an inner blue core, a series of thin white threads in the middle surrounding the core, and an outer level of translucent red backed with white bands. The red core marble on the top right obviously has a red core backed with white and can also be thought of as a tri-level, since the thin white lines are not directly on the red core but slightly distant from it, and the thin green and blue bands are much farther toward the outer edge of the marble. As stated previously, ridged core marbles with a yellow base, like the one in the upper center of Plate 11 are very scarce. The large left center marble, also about 2 $\frac{1}{4}''$ in diameter, is a very tight core, seemingly formed from a series of ribbons expertly joined together. The colors in the latter marble are also unusual, including sort of a yellow tan and a dark green and a dark red. Finally the small marble at lower left which has sort of an oblong green on yellow core (or perhaps a two lobed core if you like that term) has only two very broad red and white outer bands. These outer bands also contain flecks of mica, a combination which makes this a very rare marble.

Divided Core and Ribbon

Divided core (Plate 12) and ribbon (Plate 13) marbles are together because in some ways they are closely related. Divided core marbles also have ribbons of color near the center. However these ribbons are not nearly as wide in proportion to the marble as those which comprise the central feature of ribbon core marbles. To avoid confusion, I will refer to the sections of the divided core as strands of color rather than ribbons of color. True ribbon core marbles must have required an incredible amount of skill to make. While one can easily see how a core of clear glass could be rolled over three or four sets of colored rods to form a divided core, it is difficult to imagine how one would obtain a flat ribbon in the center of the marble using a similar technique.

Ribbon marbles come in both single and double ribbon formats. A double ribbon marble usually has two broad ribbons which parallel each other and are separated only by a little clear glass. On the other hand a divided core marble with two strands of color will have those strands swirling out opposite one another. It will come as no surprise to anyone who has collected marbles for a long time that ribbon core marbles (Plate 13) are quite rare compared with divided core marbles as a whole (Table 5-5). The vast majority of divided core marbles have either three or four strands in the center. These two groups make up 80% or more of

TABLE 5-5	RELATIVE RARITY (%) OF RIBBON AND DIVIDED CORE MARBLES BY NUMBER OF COLORED STRANDS IN THE CORE					
Marble Size	Sample Size	Ribbon	2 Str.	3 Str.	4 Str.	6 Str.
Small (≤1")	277	8%	4%	41%	47%	0%
Large (≥1⅛")	54	8%	9%	41%	39%	4%

both large and small marbles sampled. Interestingly, divided cores with only two strands or with six strands have a rarity comparable to that of ribbon marbles.

Let's take a close look at the two most common groups. In over 80% of the divided cores having three strands, each of the strands is identical in color (Table 5-6). Examples of divided core marbles with three identical strands (Plate 12) include the yellow and pink in the lower center, the red, green and blue to its immediate left, and the small (1 ½″ diameter) red and blue in the upper left. Note that the yellow and pink specimen combines unusual colors with a somewhat unusual and disorganized design, the result being the more unusual marble. Fewer three stand marbles have one of the strands differently colored. The example shown (Plate 12, lower right) has two red, white and blue strands and one red, yellow and green strand. Even fewer three strand marbles have all three strands differently colored. Two such marbles, each having one red strand, one blue strand, and one green strand are pictured on the upper right and center right of Plate 12. Note however on the center right marble that the green strand is backed with yellow, while the red and blue strands in that marble and all the strands in the upper right marble are backed with white. This small variation combined with the use of yellow outer lines on the marble with the green and yellow strand and white outer lines on the marble with the green and white strand is sufficient to give these two marbles quite a different flavor.

In contrast the most common type of four strand divided core marble has two pairs of identical strands which alternate around the marble. All three of the four strand marbles in Plate 12 are of this type (top, upper center, and center left). The marble in the upper center, the largest marble on this plate at 2 ⅜″ in diameter, may be recognized by some as the marble featured on the cover of my first edition. At least this should prove that I don't auction off all of my marbles between book

TABLE 5-6   RELATIVE RARITY (%) OF 3 AND 4 STRAND DIVIDED CORES BY NUMBERS OF IDENTICAL STRANDS

Type	Sample Size	All Alike	Two Alike	None Alike
3 Strand	22	82%	14%	4%

Type	Sample Size	All Alike	Two Pair	One Pair, Two Different
4 Strand	21	9%	67%	24%

editions! Four strand marbles in which all four strands are identical are rare. About a fourth of all four strand marbles have one paired set of strands while the two other strands which alternate with them are different from each other. Although the sample size here is small, it did not include any four strand marbles in which three strands were identical and one was different, or in which all four strands were different.

Color patterns on strands of divided core marbles are too complex and too easily changed to try to sort out into common and uncommon groupings at this point. All the glass marble maker had to do was shuffle the order of the colored rods in the iron grooves and he'd have a different color pattern on a strand. In fact this was so easy to do that I counted some marbles as having three identical strands when, in fact, the order of the colored rods was different in some of the strands. In order for strands to be counted as differently colored, either a new color had to appear or a much greater emphasis had to be put on different colors in the two strands. Another interesting variation in the color of divided core and other types of German swirls is the use of translucent colors. About 14% of the three and four strand divided core marbles had translucent colors used in the core (usually as borders on the strands) such as the reds and greens in the four strand marble at center left on Plate 12. I'll say more about the use of translucent glass when I discuss small marbles at the end of this chapter.

The second and fourth marbles in the right hand column of Plate 13 have single ribbon cores. If someone wants to know why people polish marbles, let them compare the picture of the large (2″ in diameter) ribbon core at the bottom right of Plate 13 with the picture of the same marble at center right in Plate 5 of my first edition. I don't think that there is any question that the picture in this edition shows a great deal more detail. The ribbon core, which is the only decoration in this marble, stands nearly the width of the marble itself, and is deeply bent and twisted. Such a "naked ribbon" (no outer decoration or "dressing") is currently in vogue with collectors. One half of the ribbon is yellow and one half is white. On one side a red band divides the two color halves of the ribbon, a blue stripe is centered in the yellow, and a blue-green stripe is centered on the white. On the reverse, a thin blue stripe lies in the white field and a broader green stripe on the yellow field with no dividing color band; the borders of the ribbon are edged in red. The smaller single ribbon (second from the top at right) is also intriguing. One side of the ribbon is half red and half white, and the other side of the ribbon is half blue-green and half white.

The two marbles in the center and at lower left and bottom left are all double ribbons or perhaps, in the case of the one at bottom left and upper center, two strand divided cores. The marble at top right is definitely a two strand divided core.

Actually this hair-splitting with names makes little difference, since these marbles are equally rare. The marbles at top right, upper center, and bottom left all have two ribbons which are identically colored. The one at lower left has one red on white ribbon and one green on white ribbon. The marble to its right has one red, white, yellow and green ribbon and one red, white, yellow and blue ribbon. The large marbles at top left (2 $\frac{1}{4}$" in diameter), at upper left (2 $\frac{3}{8}$" in diameter), and the small marble at lower right all display three levels of workmanship. The marble at top left has two red and one blue interior strand, one outer green strand, and two outer groups of five yellow threads, all of which are heavily twisted. Similarly the marble at upper left has two broad red, white and blue interior bands, alternating with two mid-depth and narrower red, yellow and green bands, and is again finished with two groups of five yellow threads towards the outside. The small heavily twisted marble at lower right has bright interior bands of red, blue, green, and red and yellow followed by four narrow mid-depth strands of red, and completed with a single yellow outer thread. Perhaps by that point they had simply run out of glass rods. All such types of three level workmanship make a marble more unusual than others in its general group, and should therefore command a higher price.

Lutz

Lutz marbles rank among the prized possessions of marble collectors and rightly so. Their sparkling goldstone decorations give them a brilliance that is unmatched. In my first edition goldstone marbles (as I called them) were simply classed as a variation under other types of swirls. However, Everett Grist in his book *Antique and Collectible Marbles* (1984) categorized them as a separate group. This step certainly seems justified, not only because of the value of these marbles to collectors, but also because at least some Lutz marbles (the ribbon core type) are a style which is not seen without the goldstone. Thus displaying the goldstone was the overriding factor in developing the design of the ribbon core Lutz. Lutz marbles have probably appreciated more in value than any other type of small marble since the publication of my first price guide. While most of this appreciation has been caused by their own beauty and rarity, it has also been helped by their emphasis in Grist's book and by their association with master glass maker Nicholas Lutz.

Why is there a widespread belief that marbles with goldstone were made by Nicholas Lutz? Back about the time my first edition was being published, a pamphlet came out entitled "Marbles: Identification and Price Guide" by Mel Morrison and Carl Terison. Randall and Webb (1988) give its date of publication as 1968; there is no publication date on the pamphlet itself. In this pamphlet the authors referred to goldstone marbles as Lutz marbles for the first time, and stated that Nicholas Lutz "produced copper swirls in marbles that look just like gold and still fool many people."

So who was Nicholas Lutz and did he ever make marbles? If he didn't make marbles, did he at least invent the technique that was used to produce the marbles (another widely held view)? Both of these questions can be answered with certainty.

Nicholas Lutz is one of the most well studied individuals in the glass making industry. In fact, two books suffice to tell us all we need to know about Nicholas Lutz. One is a book on sandwich glass written by Ruth Webb Lee in 1966. The second is a recent book (1987) entitled *A Guide to Sandwich Glass, Witch Balls, Containers and Toys* by Raymond Barlow and Joan Kaiser. These latter authors have researched the work of Nicholas Lutz since the 1940s and have examined documents in the Sandwich Archives and Historical Center, Sandwich Historical Society, Henry Ford Museum, and scrapbooks and records still held by the Lutz family.

They know from their research that Nicholas Lutz was born in Saint-Louis, France on February 21, 1835. His father and many of his relatives were skilled glass blowers. In 1845 at the age of ten, Nicholas was apprenticed to the Cristalleries de Saint-Louis. His apprenticeship lasted seven years after which he served four years in the French military service. Between the ages of 21 and 25 he again worked at St-Louis honing his skills in making blown glass and paperweights. At 25 he immigrated to New York City. He then worked for three different glass factories in the United States before moving to Sandwich, Massachusetts at the age of 35, and becoming the head gaffer at the Boston and Sandwich Glass Company. (A group of glass workers was called a shop and the most skilled artisan or master glass blower was referred to as the gaffer.) Lutz continued to work for the Boston and Sandwich Glass Company until a union strike forced it to close in 1887, after which Nicholas did some free-lance work and then joined the Mount Washington Glass Company and finally the Union Glass Company where he worked until his death in March of 1906.

What Nicholas Lutz produced at the Boston and Sandwich Glass Company is not only recorded in company records, but has also been documented from his home workbench. In the basement of his Sandwich home Lutz had a series of small gas burners that he used to make intricate glass items. Such work done at night at home was referred to as lamp work. Lutz's workbench had a hole in the center of it into which he could discard pieces that did not meet his standards. Discarded pieces fell into a drawer below which could be dumped out when full. Amazingly this drawer survived intact until 1984 when it became part of the Barlow collection. In the drawer were over 500 sections of rods, 1,000 leaves, petals and fruit for paperweights, completed paperweights with defects, writing pens, cigar holders, and hands for leather dolls. There were also footballs, birds, and crosses that could be used in paperweights or as finials on pens. However nowhere in the contents of the drawer or in the records of the Boston and Sandwich Glass Factory are there any marbles.

What Lutz did make were glass flowers and paperweights in which such flowers were a decoration. On November 7, 1887 Lutz's shop made 150 such weights. He also made fruit paperweights, blown vases with paperweight bases, blown lamps, decorative pipes, flasks, creamers, tumblers, wafer trays, threaded creamers, threaded double handled tankers, writing pens, champagne and wine glasses, and even added decorations to blown cigar holders. (The latter was a free-lance job done at home.) Again, in all this extensive documentation, no mention is made of marbles. Ruth Webb Lee's book includes a letter written by Victor Lutz, Nicholas's son, about his father: "He specialized in fancy colored glass, nappies (a shallow bowl) and bowls for cutting, chandelier arms and thin glass in stem work. Also he did considerable work at the old home here. He had a workshop set up with tallow lamp and made different kinds of fruits and flowers, etc. for paperweights for the Boston and Sandwich Glass Company. For his friends he made threaded pens, flasks, paperweights, cigarette holders, and many fancy articles of different designs."

Because of the extensive research done on Nicholas Lutz and because of the fortunate acquisition of his workbench it seems clear that not only were marbles never a production item with either Nicholas Lutz or the Boston and Sandwich Glass Company, but that Nicholas Lutz never made any marbles, even as part of his lamp work at home.

If Nicholas Lutz did not make any goldstone marbles, then was he responsible for the technique of using gold aventurine or glass having copper filings to decorate other glass items? The four major techniques attributed to Nicholas Lutz by Barlow and Kaiser (1987) include making paperweights, threaded glass made by winding colored threads around the outside of thinly blown clear glass, making clear hollow glassware such as wafer trays with colored threads incorporated in the clear glass in a swirl configuration, and combining ribbons of colored glass in clear glass hollow-ware to make swirled stripes. (Note that none of this mentions aventurine glass or goldstone). Some aventurine glass is attributed to the Boston and Sandwich Glass Company, but I have not seen any authenticated pieces using aventurine glass which are attributed to Nicholas Lutz. Even though Lutz did not make or develop the technique for goldstone marbles, the name Lutz marble is too well established to fight. Nor is "Lutz-type" any better, since Lutz did not make a "type" like that. Names do not need to indicate a maker and Lutz marbles are here to stay.

If Lutz marbles weren't produced at the Boston and Sandwich Glass Factory, then where and when were they produced? Fortunately we have some very good information on this, since these marbles are clearly featured in Butler Brothers catalogs from the early 1900s. Butler Brothers, a wholesale firm whose name later changed to City Products Corporation, clearly differentiated in their catalogs between American made marbles and imported marbles. The "fancy gold band glass marble assortment" is definitely listed under imported marbles. They are listed along with latticinio core and sulphide marbles and therefore presumably came from Germany as well. The same marbles are referred to in a William Croft and Sons Toronto catalog as "crystal gold band alleys."

The Butler Brothers catalog is very specific as to the types of Lutz marbles offered in their box of 100. There were four styles each in five colors. These styles included one referred to as "opal" with fine colored stripes and gold bands and another referred to as "transparent" with the same decoration. The other two styles are a black opaque with gold stripes and fine colored stripes, and a colored transparent with an opaque spiral center, stripes and gold bands (ie. a ribbon core Lutz). Prices for the smaller sizes and the years in which they were offered are given in Table 5-7. The final listing in that table is from an undated portion of a Butler Brothers catalog. I presume from the price that the date would be 1915. Since these marbles originally were not very expensive, they were sometimes used in advertising signs. A large number were pried out of a concrete matrix in a bank sign taken down on Wellington, Texas. Some of these marbles are now owned by

TABLE 5-7　PRICES FOR LUTZ MARBLES IN WHOLESALE AND RETAIL CATALOGS
FROM THE EARLY 1900S

Catalog	Year	Price per 100		
		Size 0 ($\frac{9}{16}$")	Size 1 ($\frac{5}{8}$")	Size 2 ($\frac{3}{4}$")
Butler Brothers	1910	0.35	0.45	0.55
Wm. Croft and Sons	1912	0.50	0.60	0.80
Butler Brothers	1914	0.39	0.50	0.60
Butler Brothers	1915	0.40	0.50	0.60

Wholesale - Butler Brothers, later City Products Corp. Retail - Wm. Croft and Sons.

J.E. McGuire in Oklahoma. For a final bit of proof regarding the manufacture of goldstone marbles and Nicholas Lutz, note that the catalog listings for these marbles occur between the years 1910 and 1914. Nicholas Lutz, you will recall, died in 1906.

Information on the history of aventurine glass is supplied in the book *19th Century Glass* by Albert Revi (1959). Revi uses a definition by Professor E. Peligot of France who said: "Aventurine is a yellowish glass in which there are an infinite number of small crystals of copper, protoxide of copper, or silicate of that oxide. When it is polished, this glass presents, especially in the light, a glittering appearance for which reason it is used in jewelry." The Venetians are credited with the discovery of aventurine. They had long used the technique of combining rods of aventurine with intricately designed filigree glassware. Even when chemists and glass makers in France developed an imitation of the original product between the years 1860 and 1865, they were not able to produce aventurine with the true golden color typical of the Venetian product. Glass rods of aventurine have been supplied to glass houses all over the world by the Dalla Venenzia family of Venice for a period of over 200 years. Such rods were probably ordered from Venice by both the German marble factories and by the Boston and Sandwich Glass Company.

If these marbles were manufactured relatively late in the second decade of the 1900s, and if they were priced fairly inexpensively and sold in lots of 100, why are they so rare and valuable today? Although this is speculation, I imagine that timing was crucial here. The technique for making these marbles wasn't developed until shortly before World War I. The war would have interrupted the production of these marbles, both through stopping the importation of aventurine (it is unlikely that the German factories produced their own) and through the interruption in toy making while manufacturers tried to help the war effort. As we have seen, handmade marbles continued to be produced in Germany after the war, but only those that could compete cheaply with the machine-made marbles in the United States. The goldstone rods were probably now too costly for the German toy makers to purchase. Thus, while latticinio cores continued to be produced, the Lutz marbles were no longer made. If this was the case, then these marbles may only have been produced for about six years, making them rarer today than other types that were produced in lesser amounts per year, but were sold over a much longer period of time.

Goldstone was never used as part of the core or interior decoration in any marble which was a regular production item at the factories, although some goldstone is present as part of a wispy, divided core in a clear mica marble (1 $\frac{1}{4}$″) owned by the Frank Amrheins in New York. The luster in goldstone is liable to be lost if it is worked at too hot a temperature or reheated too often. Apparently, goldstone was easiest to use by scattering crushed bits of it among the other bits of crushed glass used to make onionskin marbles. This process will be discussed in the section on onionskins in this chapter. Thus it should come as no great surprise that multi-colored onionskin marbles represent the most common type of Lutz (see Table 5-8 and Plate 14). Some of the marble makers probably found very quickly that the goldstone would be more spectacular and show up better against a single colored background. Thus single color onionskins with Lutz make up about 17% of the Lutz type as a group (Plate 14, top, center, and center right). I have seen four different colors used as single color backgrounds in Lutz marbles: white, which is the most common (Plate 14, top and large marble top left, 1 $\frac{7}{8}$″ in diameter) yellow and green, which are less common than white (Plate 14, in

TABLE 5-8   RELATIVE RARITY (%) OF LUTZ MARBLES BY STYLE

Sample Size	Coreless Swirl	Colored Swirl	Opaque Swirl	Ribbon Core	Single Color Onion	Multiple Color Onion
106	25%	12%	7%	10%	17%	29%

spheroidals box and marbles in front of box); and black, which in my experience is the rarest. Another common design using Lutz marbles is to have swirls of Lutz near the surface. Such marbles in clear glass (Plate 15, lower circle, large center marble 2 $\frac{1}{8}$″ in diameter) are about twice as common as those in colored glass (see Table 5-8 and Plate 15, upper circle). On about the same order of rarity as the colored glass swirls are ribbon core Lutz marbles (Plate 14, upper right, outer circle). The rarest category, as one might expect, are opaque marbles having swirls of Lutz at the surface (Plate 15, upper circle, center two and lower four). As can be seen on Plate 15, the clear banded Lutz come in a variety of colors as do the colored banded and opaque banded. Undoubtedly some colors are rarer than others. My sample size is not large enough to make these distinctions, except to say that blue is a relatively common color for the outer swirls on the clear glass variety.

Colored Glass and Coreless Swirls

Colored glass marbles deserve to be discussed as a separate group since, like Lutz, colored glass marbles require unique designs for decoration. Colored glass made the use of colored ribbons within the glass impossible, since the interior colors either couldn't be seen at all or wound up looking brown or gray. Thus colored glass marbles had to be decorated either with bands or swirls of white near the surface, or with color put on the surface as an overlay, like that used with opaque marbles. Coreless swirls are (as the name implies) clear glass marbles without a core. These are generally decorated in styles typically used for colored glass or opaque glass, and thus are discussed here. Coreless swirls are uncommon since colored glass provided a better contrast with overlay or outer decorations. Colored marbles themselves are uncommon because, like most other rarities, they didn't work out well as a production item.

Just how rare are colored marbles? Even though I've always been a little biased toward colored glass, I will use my own collection statistics. Thus, if anything, colored glass should appear overly numerous in the tables. If we lump all opaque marbles together and all colored glass marbles together, both are more common than the Lutz type (Table 5-9). If we split opaques into white glass and black glass and colored marbles into internal decoration and near surface or overlay decoration, then Lutz, black glass opaques, and surface decorated colored glass marbles are about equally common, while white glass opaques and colored

TABLE 5-9   RELATIVE RARITY (%) OF COLORED GLASS, LUTZ, AND OPAQUE GLASS MARBLES (SAMPLE SIZE = 367)

Lutz	Opaque		Colored	
	Total		Total	
24%	40%		36%	
Lutz	Black	White	Internal	Surface or Near Surface
24%	26%	14%	9%	27%

marbles with interior decorations are rarer. Of course we could divide the Lutz marbles into types, as we could divide the black and white opaque marbles into types and the colored glass marbles into types. Thus rarity depends upon how you split and lump categories of marbles.

There is nothing quite so striking as placing a colored glass marble where it can be lit from behind. Unfortunately large specimens of colored glass are particularly rare, and thus the opportunities for that sort of display are quite limited. Rarity within the colored glass group was determined, as it usually is, by the success of the marble in the marketplace. Thus the maypole marbles, in which white or yellow threads or thin colored bands are swirled around the marble either on the surface (overlay) or just barely underneath the surface, make up the largest category (Table 5-10). Examples include the amber, lavender, and green marbles (Plate 16, above center) which have sparse threads of yellow or white; the blue marbles (Plate 16, lower left) some of which have two colors of threads; and the marbles at the bottom right of Plate 17 which have bicolored bands. Blue is the most common glass color for maypole marbles (50%). These were successful, since

TABLE 5-10   RELATIVE RARITY (%) OF COLORED GLASS MARBLES BY TYPE (SAMPLE SIZE = 131)

Maypole	Gooseberry	Ribbon	Core & Swirl	Colored Indian	Submarine	Other
32%	18%	18%	7%	8%	8%	9%

the combination of surface color and colored glass produced a fairly attractive marble.

Similarly the gooseberry and amber ribbon styles were also fairly successful. Gooseberries were really a colored glass clambroth style with numerous thin white threads spaced evenly around the marble's surface. Named gooseberry because of the design and the predominance of amber glass (90%), this type also comes in blue glass and clear glass (Plate 17, center right). The clear glass version, of course, could also be classified as an open core swirl. Amber ribbons have a large white ribbon near the surface in amber glass (Plate 17, lower left). I have only seen a single marble of this style in another color of glass (purple).

Another major group of colored glass marbles is that characterized by having broader bands of outer, overlay color on the surface. Decorations on these sometimes imitate the overlay on Indian marbles, but more variety seems to be present on these "banded transparents" (Plate 16, upper left). The same decoration is also used on clear glass marbles, forming attractive and unusual marbles which could be referred to as a type of coreless swirl. In fact this type of broad band overlay is found on marbles ranging from clear to lightly colored glass (Plate 16, lower right and bottom) to glass dark enough to need a strong light to show the color (Plate 16, upper right). Such "Indian" style marbles which have a colored glass dark enough to appear opaque even in brightly lit rooms, but still transparent enough to allow a strong light to pass through, I've termed "mag-lites." Many collectors use the small, powerful Mag-Lite flashlights to illuminate these marbles and to distinguish them from the truly opaque Indians. Mag-lites thus complete the continuum from colored glass with overlay through Indians. In my opinion mag-lites are rarer than truly opaque Indians. Colors of mag-lite marbles include purple (by far the most common), green, and red.

Colored glass marbles with internal decoration such as a solid core, deeply imbedded white swirls, or a latticinio core comprise only 7% of the colored glass marble total (Table 5-10), even when lumped together (under core and swirl marbles). This is because these sorts of decorations usually did not work out well; the inner designs were very difficult to see in colored glass. A solid or divided core in colored glass (Plate 17, upper left) did not really enhance the appearance of the marble very much. Similarly the more traditional style latticinio marbles (Plate 17, center and center left) did not work well in color either. Note how the red bands in the large marble at center left (Plate 17) are darkened by the amber glass. Even the use of white swirls or a white core and swirls (Plate 17, upper center, right), while being very attractive in the larger green glass marble are almost completely hidden in the blue glass marble above it. Large swirls in colored glass are at least as rare as sulphides in colored glass.

Another rare group are the marbles that collectors have been calling submarines. These consist of some inner color near the surface as well as some outer, overlay color. The examples in Plate 16 (center left) include (right to left) a green and two blues; note how bands of white can be seen underneath the colored glass. The "other" category includes both marbles with no decoration at all (Plate 17, bottom left), and marbles which look more like the slag or imitation onyx style produced later by semi-automated and automated processes. This latter group may have been produced in America (probably during the 1890s or 1900s) rather than in Germany.

Mist

Mist marbles have not previously been described as a distinct group. One reason is their scarcity and another is the ease with which they can be misidentified if handled quickly. Mist marbles are positioned after colored glass because, in effect, they are an imitation colored glass marble. When seen at a distance these marbles appear to be colored glass marbles. In fact, I have purchased them at auctions under the impression that I was bidding on colored glass marbles, and have been pleasantly surprised to find that I had a mist marble instead.

The marbles are made primarily of clear glass and the color is given to them by very thin streaks of colored glass which are densely distributed toward the outside of the marble and which usually completely surround the marble (Plate 18A, upper half). These tiny streaks remind me of a curtain of mist, the type of thing you might see just beyond a large waterfall. Mist marbles appear to come in two basic varieties. One of these is decorated with outer overlay bands (often a single color) in the same maypole design often used for colored glass marbles. The second variety has no outer decoration but contains a sprinkling of mica flecks. Thus the makers of these marbles must have thought that they needed either mica or outer decoration to make them interesting enough to sell. Some collectors refer to these marbles as "lined micas," but this term is misleading, since the method used to produce mist marbles was different and more involved than that used for micas.

Apparently the colored mist was not formed by using colored glass rods, but by using finely crushed pieces of colored glass and then pulling the rod until these turned into streaks. In other words they were made by the same technique used to make onionskin marbles. Was this design developed to save money by using less of the presumably more expensive colored glass in each marble? We may never know. What we do know is that these marbles are difficult to find and can be considered quite rare. I have only seen three colors of mist marbles; blue seems to be most common, green less common, and yellow very uncommon.

Opaque Glass

Opaque glass marbles have always held a special fascination for collectors. Their rarity and beauty have combined to make them one of the centers of anyone's marble collection. They also present a nightmare to anybody writing a marble book, since an assortment of different names have been given to the different types over the years. Sometimes the same marbles were called different things in different regions. One of earliest of these names, the clambroth, was given to white opaque marbles having evenly spaced thin lines of color around the outside. The confusion starts when one wants to name a white opaque marble with broad bands of color or a black opaque marble with thin, evenly spaced outer lines. Are the broad banded whites a different type of clambroth? Most collectors don't seem to think so. How about the black ones, are they a black clambroth? After all, clambroth or clam chowder might be white or even red but never black! However most collectors have adopted this terminology so I am going to "go with the flow" and take the easy way out. Following what seems to have become the common convention I will use the thin, evenly spaced lines of outer color to designate a clambroth, no matter what the base color of the marble is. Thus we have white clambroths, black clambroths, etc. On the other hand those marbles with broad bands of overlay color will be referred to as banded opaques. Again there are white banded opaques and black banded opaques, which are referred to as Indians. There are also opaque marbles with different base colors. Most of these are pastel shades of blue, yellow, purple, or green. I'm going to refer to these marbles as pastels, even though some of them have a darker or more vivid hue. Marbles of this type with bands of color on the surface are "banded pastels" and those with the clambroth design are "pastel clams." Numerically, Indian marbles dominate the opaque marble category as a whole (Table 5-11). White clambroths as a group make up another quarter of the opaque marbles. Banded whites are less common as are black clambroths, and all pastel marbles are quite rare.

TABLE 5-11   RELATIVE RARITY (%) OF OPAQUE GLASS MARBLES WITH OVERLAY BY TYPE (SAMPLE SIZE = 616)

White		Black			Pastel
Clam	Banded	Clam	Banded (Indian)	Other	All
25%	10%	5%	54%	3%	3%

Before we leave terminology we have to say something about the name Indian. Again, it was Morrison and Terison's little book that first used the name "Indian Swirl" for black banded opaque marbles. Their section on Indian Swirls states that "This variation of the swirl marble was made only in India, all through the 1800s . . . and never imported, but only brought back by tourists, etc.

I have never seen a shred of evidence to support this statement. In the mid or even late 1800s America still had a wild west, commercial air travel didn't exist, and tourism to India was not exactly a big time operation. (Talk about a slow boat trip!) It seems completely unlikely that "tourists" could have brought back the number of these marbles which have been found in the United States. India itself was a colony in the British empire until 1947, and was known largely for exports of things such as rubber, rice, and tea, not glass or glass objects. Why anyone in India, either foreign or native, would set up a factory to produce glass marbles, much less glass marbles made only of black glass and requiring an overlay, boggles the mind. These marbles were probably produced in Germany as were the other types of cane cut marbles. As we have seen, black glass opaques come in the clambroth style and white glass opaques come in the banded style; there is no reason to suspect these were made in different countries. However the name Indian, like the name Lutz, has caught on among collectors. (Hopefully because the marble evokes images of bright native fabrics on a dark jungle continent.) In any event the name is now well established. Perhaps calling these marbles Indians isn't really such a bad mistake; after all, even Christopher Columbus had problems with the name Indian.

The information on relative rarity within the clambroth pattern was compiled both from my own collection and from surveys made at the Amana Marble Show and the Columbus Marble Show (Table 5-12). Due to my lack of detail in the survey, multi-colored clams other than red and blue are lumped together as a group. Also missing entirely from the table are numbers of pastel clams (represented on Plate 19 by the two blue marbles upper center), and any black glass

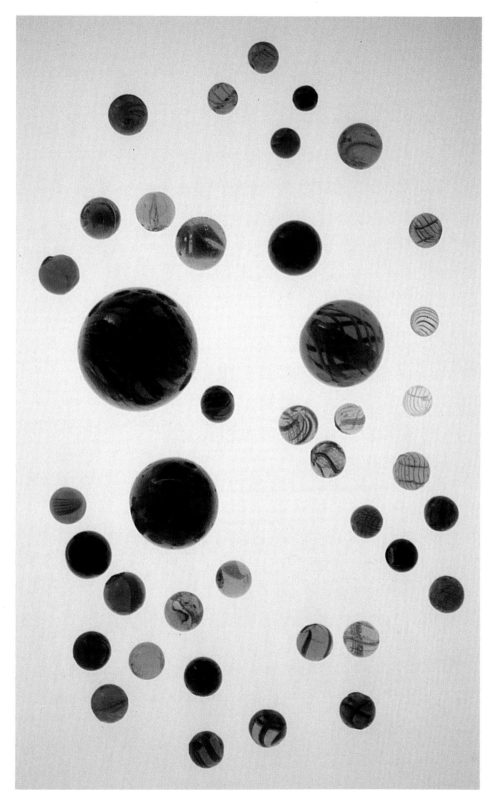

Plate 17. Colored Glass with Inner Decoration.

Plate 18A. Mist Marbles.

Plate 18B. Peppermint, Ballot Box Marbles, and Pastels.

Plate 19. Clambroths.

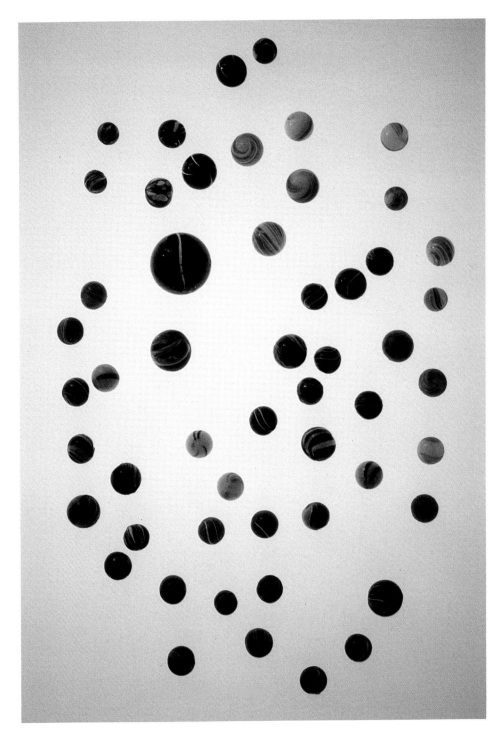

Plate 20. Banded Opaques and Indians.

Plate 21. Mica Marbles.

Plate 22. Segmented Onionskins.

Plate 23. Non-Segmented Onionskins.

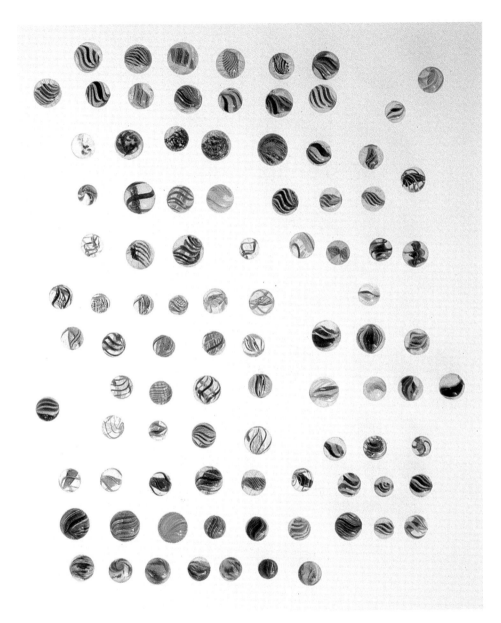

Plate 24. A Variety of Small Swirls.

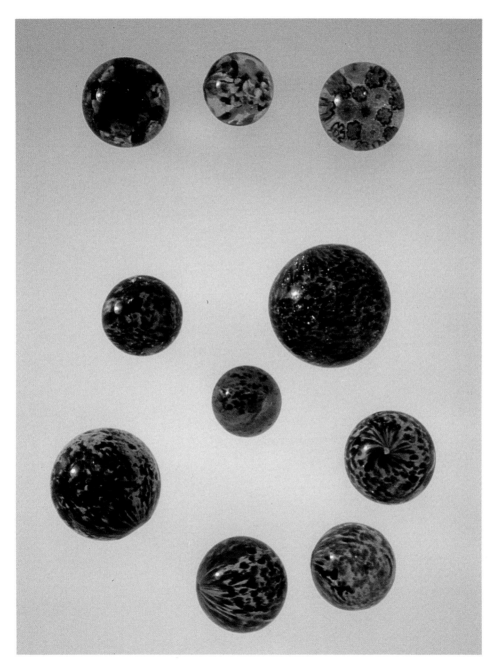

Plate 25. End-of-Day, Cloud, and Paperweight.

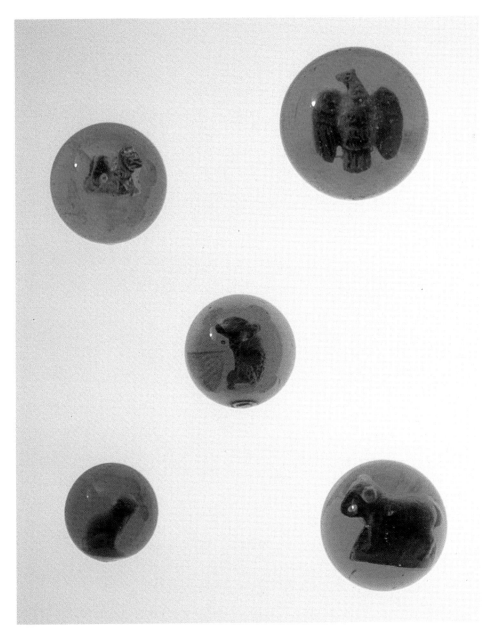

Plate 26. Sulphides in Colored Glass.

Plate 27. Colored Figure Sulphides.

Plate 28A. Roman Glass Marbles.

Plate 28B. Tri-Color Horse Sulphide.

Plate 28C. Mark Matthews Marbles.

Plate 28D. Latticinio Ribbons and Banded Latticinio.

Plate 28E. Orange/White and Orange/Yellow Latticinio.

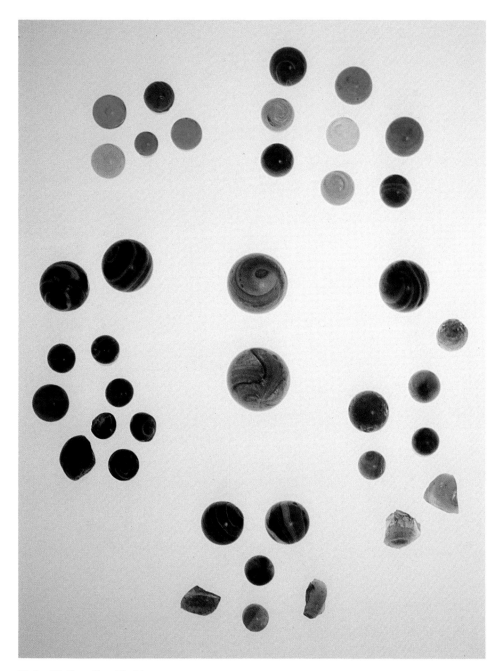

Plate 29. Transition Marbles.

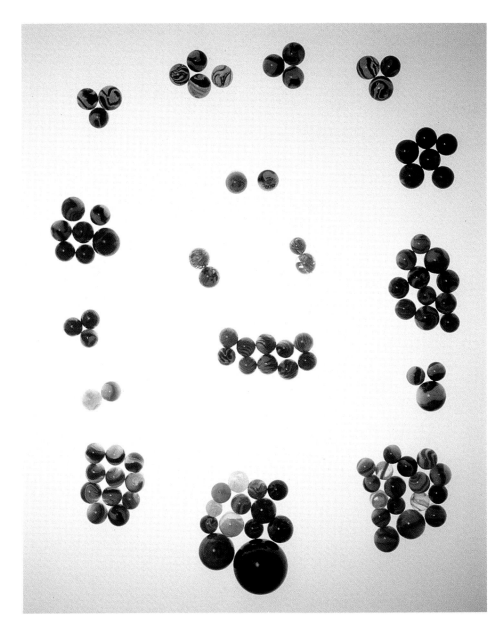

Plate 30. Machine-Made Marbles.

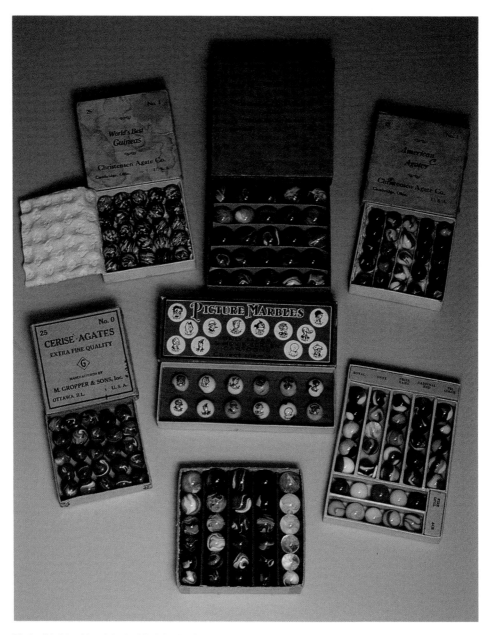

Plate 31. Machine-Made Marbles in Original Boxes.

Plate 32. Marble Games.

TABLE 5-12　RELATIVE RARITY (%) OF CLAMBROTH BY COLOR PATTERN
　　　　　　(SAMPLE SIZE = 154)

Red	Blue	Green	Other Single	Red and Blue	Other Multi-Colored	White on Black
24%	24%	11%	2%	8%	15%	16%

clams having the outer decoration in a color other than white. Examples of the latter in Plate 19 include the yellow, orange, blue, and yellow and white striped marbles at center left. However both the pastels and the non-white decorated blacks are extremely rare. Red or blue clams on the white glass are the most common (Table 5-12, Plate 19, center and lower left). These are followed in order by white decorated black glass (Plate 19, bottom right) and green decorated white glass (Plate 19, center right). The largest of the black clams (Plate 19, lower right) is 2 ⅛″ in diameter. White glass clams with red and blue stripes (Plate 19, upper right) are only slightly less common than the green single striped clams. Among the other multi-colored clam groups, those having red, blue, and green alternating around the marble (Plate 19, upper left) are almost as common as those just having red and blue. On the other hand marbles containing yellow (Plate 19, upper right) or brown are quite scarce.

　　Bands on white opaques are predominately red (see Table 5-13 and Plate 20, upper center-right), with blue and red and blue being much harder to find (Plate 20, upper right). Other combinations, such as those with yellow or green, are scarcer yet. Indians are more difficult to break into groups than white banded opaques, because more colors were used in the bands on the Indian marbles. Indians can be divided into two sub-groups according to whether or not the bands are outlined in white. Those with bands outlined are less common than those

TABLE 5-13　RELATIVE RARITY OF BANDED OPAQUE MARBLES
　　　　　　(SAMPLE SIZE = 50 BANDED WHITE, 74 INDIAN)

Banded White				Indian	
Red	Blue	Red & Blue	Other	White Outline	Other
66%	10%	16%	8%	38%	62%

where the bands are not outlined. The most common color combination in both groups is having one band in a blue color and one in a red or orange color. However a great variation in both color shades and amounts of color occur on Indian marbles, and the research needed to sort these into subgroups by rarity has not been done. Some black glass opaques lumped in the other category in Table 5-11 have lines or spots of bright color covering the entire marble. These "gaudy blacks" (Plate 20, two small marbles at upper far left) are much rarer than the banded varieties. I should also note here that some of the marbles pictured as Indians in Plate 20 are really "mag-lites" since they are transparent enough to show their purple, red, or green color in a strong flashlight beam. These marble types grade into one another and are discussed more extensively in the colored glass section.

Banded pastels run the gamut from pinks to reds, yellows to mustards, light greens and blues to bright blues and dark greens. Remember, for marbles with overlay and a base color other than black or white: if it's opaque it's a pastel, if it's colored glass it's a banded transparent, if it's clear it's an open core swirl, and if it's translucent you can call it whatever you want! Banded pastels circle from left to right in the central lower two-thirds of Plate 20. Notice that the outer bands on these are often bicolored.

Undecorated opaques (Plate 18B, right circle) come primarily in white and black (circle center). The predominance of these two colors is because of their use as ballot box marbles (see Ballot Box section in Chapter 8). As one might expect in such a case, white ballot box marbles are more common than black. Undecorated pastels come in a wide variety of hues including pinks and reds (30%), blues (40%), yellows (9%), greens (17%), and purples (4%). We really know very little about the production of these marbles (other than the fact that they were cut from canes) or their use. It is tempting to think that pastels were used in early games similar to the later Chinese checkers games that required numbers of solidly colored marbles.

Peppermints/Flags

Peppermint marbles are not formed of opaque glass but consist of a clear core of glass surrounded by a thin layer of white glass. The white glass is usually decorated with broad blue bands and red stripes (Plate 18B, left circle). These marbles vary chiefly in the number of red stripes between the blue bands. Marbles with one, two, and three stripes all seem about equally common. Mica flecks are rarely added to the blue field (bottom of circle), and large marbles of this type such as the one at the circle's center ($1\frac{5}{8}''$ diameter) are extremely rare. There are marbles with other decorations made by the same technique. The two on either side of the mica peppermint have the same white base layer over clear, but have evenly spaced red lines on the white, a sort of clambroth effect. It is not a "cased opaque" because it is not an opaque marble; it has a clear glass core. While some true "cased opaque" marbles probably exist, i.e. those having a layer of clear glass over a regular opaque glass marble, they would be extremely rare. The red, white, and blue peppermints first discussed are listed in a 1912 William Croft and Sons catalog as flag allies. It is somewhat interesting that this is a Canadian catalog featuring a "flag alley" with colors from the U.S. flag. A box of 100 in the $\frac{5}{8}''$ size sold for $1.00 and a box of 100 in the $\frac{3}{4}''$ size sold for $1.40.

Mica

A jar full of mica marbles is a real showcase delight. A little side lighting will cause the colors to glow and the mica to sparkle. Mica marbles were produced over a long period of time, being part of a picture frame dated 1869, and come in a full range of colors and hues (Plate 21). Thus designations as to rarity depend upon how finely we lump or split the assorted colors. I decided in this instance to be a "lumper" rather than a "splitter." Clear marbles, including those with a slight bluish tinge (Plate 21, center), and blue marbles including turquoise (Plate 21, upper left) are both relatively common (Table 5-14). Greens (Plate 21, top) and ambers, including yellow (Plate 21, upper right) are slightly less common but still abundant. That leaves us with the 5% in our "other" category. Red micas (Plate 21, bottom) are the "in thing" these days; everybody knows how scarce they are.

TABLE 5-14   RELATIVE RARITY (%) OF MICA MARBLES BY COLOR (SAMPLE SIZE = 286)

Clear and Bluish	Blue and Turquoise	Green	Amber and Yellow	Other
28%	27%	22%	18%	5%

However reds are only one of at least five rare color types (refer to Plate 21) which include: fire amber, violet (mid row, lower center), a blue-green which appears gray (above amber), a vaseline color (lower center), and a smoky color which appears almost black (lower center, right). All of these color groups would be 1% or less of the total number of micas looked at, and some may be rarer than the reds, although it's hard to tell with such small numbers. These colors are rare for one of two reasons: either the colors themselves were expensive or hard to produce, or, as is the case with the blue-green/grays, violets, and smokies, the final appearance of the marble was dark and unattractive and little mica could be seen. In my first edition I referred to micas as "snowflakes." I thought this might have been a term used solely by my father and me, but mica marbles are clearly labeled as "snowflakes" in an early article in *Harpers Young People* magazine (Roberts, 1883).

Onionskin

Onionskin marbles are cane cut swirls which are solidly colored instead of having ribbons or threads of color in clear glass. However the solid color on these marbles is not the result of an opaque glass core, but is rather created by a thin layer of color (base color) surrounding an inner clear core. Apparently this style of marble was produced almost from the beginning of the cane cut glass marble industry. A pink onionskin was found in an archaeological excavation of a privy in the Irish Channel area of New Orleans, and was dated to 1850–1860 (Gartley and Carskadden, 1987). Furthermore four segmented onionskins were used to decorate the frame of an oil painting which had the date 1869 spelled out using Indian corn.

The base color, usually white or yellow, was probably formed by rolling a clear glass center in powdered white or yellow glass. (See beginning of this chapter.) The white glass which was used in the antique marbles, by the way, got its brightness from the inclusion of arsenic in the glass. Even recent white rods of glass coming from Germany can contain up to 20% arsenic. The accent colors were applied to the base color by rolling the hot glass rod over pieces of crushed glass. Such pieces, usually red, blue, or green, could be evenly mixed or arranged by color in groups or segments and rolled on in some sort of sequential order. Some marbles, particularly large ones, have what appears to be alternating sections of base colors (white with yellow). In reality the yellow is probably applied prior to the accent color as powdered glass, i.e. there is probably a base white layer under the yellow. When the rod was fired and coated with clear glass the red, blue, and green crushed glass formed spots or dots of color. The old German makers referred to onionskins as "speckled" marbles.

If the rod was then pulled into a cane, these spots or dots of color started to turn into streaks or lines of color. The more the cane was pulled the more completely the dots turned into streaks. This can be seen on large marbles which were pulled very little; these marbles have spots near the center and streaks near the ends that were pulled or twisted. Small diameter marbles, on the other hand, are seldom spotted and usually have nothing but streaks or lines. The suggestion has been made (Grist, 1988) that small onionskin type marbles where the color has been pulled into lines should be regarded as a separate type and called opaque swirls. Since, as just explained, these marbles were produced by exactly the same methods as those having spots, and since a full gradation of types can be found, there seems to be no reason to create another category. Whether there are spots or lines depends completely on how much the rod was pulled after the crushed glass was applied to the base.

Most onionskin marbles can be grouped into one of three categories: those with differently colored segments (Plate 22); those that appear to be a single color, at least when viewed from a distance (Plate 23); and those that are speckled or spotted, usually with at least two colors (Plate 23). (A few larger onionskins have spots of a single color on a white or yellow background.) For Table 5-15 I have termed all of those which have only a single color glass on a base color as "single color" marbles; only spotted marbles having at least two colors are listed under the "speckled" category (Plate 23, lower left). These marbles vary considerably in the density of color added to the white base and in the size of the crushed glass chunks used. The largest marble at the top of the speckled group is $2\frac{1}{2}''$ in diameter.

TABLE 5-15   RELATIVE RARITY (%) OF ONIONSKIN MARBLES BY TYPE
(SAMPLE SIZE = 79 LARGE, 180 SMALL)

Large			Small		
Segmented	Single Color	Speckled	Segmented	Single Color	Speckled
68%	22%	10%	55%	44%	1%

Segmented marbles are the most common variety in both the large and small sizes (Table 5-15). In the large size, single colored marbles are much less common than segmented marbles. In the small size category, however, single colored marbles, while being somewhat more unusual than segmented marbles, are also quite common. This is logical, since a single color in a small marble is attractive, but a single color on a large marble might be too plain to hold the attention of a potential buyer. Note also in Table 5-15 that speckled marbles, while rare in both categories, are more numerous as large marbles than as small marbles. Again this is logical since, as mentioned earlier, pulling a rod down to a small size would change the spots into lines. Thus to make a small marble with spots would require extra effort on the part of the glass artisan.

If we look at the largest category, segmented onionskins, and subdivide them by color pattern, we find that red and blue segments alternating on a white base are the most common for both large and small marbles (see Table 5-16 and Plate 22, upper left, center, and right). Similarly blue on white alternating with red on yellow (or red and yellow on white) is the second most common marble in the small size, and is tied for second in the large size (Plate 22, lower left and lower right). Next in line comes red alternating with green on a base of white (Plate 22, upper right), this marble being in third place among small marbles and tied for second among large marbles. All other color arrangements, such as red alternating with both blue and green (Plate 22, center left) are much less common. The 26% "other" category in large marbles is caused by a large number of different types in which white and yellow base colors alternate, for example the red/white, red/yellow marble ($2\frac{1}{8}''$ diameter) at the bottom of Plate 22. However (with the exception of the previously mentioned red on yellow and blue on white) even the most common of these patterns, red on white alternating with green on yellow,

TABLE 5-16	**RELATIVE RARITY (%) OF SEGMENTED ONIONSKINS BY COLOR** (SAMPLE SIZE = 34 LARGE, 99 SMALL)						
	R/B	R/G	R/B/G	B/G	R/B	R/G	
	W	W	W	W	Y/W	Y	Other
Large	26%	18%	3%	6%	18%	3%	26%
Small	30%	16%	5%	4%	25%	12%	7%

Letters below line indicate base color; R = red, B = blue, G = green, Y = yellow, W = white.

occurs in only 6% of the specimens looked at. However, note that the sample size on large onionskins is quite small and probably does not accurately represent differences among the rarer categories.

For single color onionskins I only determined relative rarity for the smaller sized marbles, since there were too few large ones to be examined. Somewhat surprisingly blue on white ranks most common (Plate 23, upper center) followed by red on yellow (Table 5-17). Note that the three red on yellow marbles in Plate 23 (left center to top) were subjected to different amounts of pulling (spots versus lines) and that all three show touches of green glass. The inclusion of small pieces of a third color is not unusual and does not change the marble's category. Red on white (Plate 23, upper center right) and green on white (Plate 23, center right, $2\frac{1}{2}''$ in diameter) are somewhat scarcer and green on yellow is very uncommon (Plate 23, lower right). There isn't an "other" category because these were the only color patterns that I saw. Thus at least in the regular playing size, this type of onionskin was apparently made in a fairly limited number of colors.

Unusual onionskins include those that are lobed (Plate 23, lower center). Lobes in onionskin marbles are usually rounded, unlike the sharp-edged ridges seen in solid cores. Numbers of lobes can vary from two to sixteen. Such lobed onionskins are quite unusual and much rarer than the normal variety. Another rarity is a segmented onionskin with six segments rather than the usual four. The latter marble is one of those foolers; when you look at it it appears a little different, but unless you concentrate you'll miss the reason why.

Of course the addition of mica to an onionskin also enhances its value. Sometimes the mica was applied right along with the colored glass flecks and appears to be part of the color pattern. Marbles made in this style include the speckled marble at the bottom center of Plate 23, and the red/yellow, red/white and red/yellow, and blue/white onionskins in the lower right of Plate 22. The

TABLE 5-17   RELATIVE RARITY (%) OF SINGLE COLORED ONIONSKINS BY COLOR (SAMPLE SIZE = 79 SMALL MARBLES)

B	R	G	R	G
W	W	W	Y	Y
35%	19%	16%	25%	4%

Letters below line indicate base color; R = red, B = blue, G = green, Y = yellow, W = white.

latter marble also has four lobes. The small red and blue marble in the upper center of Plate 22 also has mica flecks as well as greenish crystals. Other times the mica was applied in a separate layer after clear had been added over the top of the color layer. The red/yellow ($1\frac{7}{8}''$ diameter) and blue/white ($2''$ diameter) in the upper left and right respectively of Plate 23 were made with this "double layer" technique. Finally we have the small green and blue marble (Plate 22, upper left) in which the green itself sparkles because it is green aventurine.

Joseph Swirls

I have chosen to discuss Joseph swirls with onionskins, since at a quick glance they appear to be onionskins. However, these marbles were made with colored rods, not with powdered or ground pieces of glass. In other words, the manufacturing process was very similar to that used for other types of swirl marbles. Joseph swirls have a clear glass core with no interior decoration. A continuous series of colored rods was then added around the outside of the marble, and covered with another thin layer of clear. Thus the marble gives the appearance of being solid colored around the outside like an onionskin, an effect caused by the colored rods being laid next to one another all the way around the marble (Plate 23, center left). Joseph swirls can be very colorful, and the name presumably derives from Joseph's Coat of Many Colors mentioned in the Old Testament. Joseph swirls are quite rare compared to onionskins. Very few of them showed up in my collection. Joseph swirls are also closely related to other types of open core swirls with outer decoration. Swirls of this type were also part of the decoration on the picture frame dated 1869. Thus we know that such marbles were produced in some of the earlier years of antique marble production.

Small Swirls

One of the very best bargains available today are small swirl marbles. Apparently a lot of advanced collectors feel that the best way for a young collector with a limited budget to spend his money is on the later machine-made marbles which still go for a couple of dollars apiece. While this isn't necessarily a bad choice, much older handmade marbles (the small glass swirls) often sell for a comparable price. At large marble auctions the big wheeler-dealers often battle it out with mega-bucks over the large and rare pieces up for sale. By the end of the auction these folks are all tired, broke, and disinterested. About this time all the auctioneer has left are a few benningtons, clays, and small swirls (bagged in groups of 10 or 20 or more) which he would like to unload in a hurry. The only competition for these marbles are a few flea market dealers who need to buy at wholesale prices. Don't expect to find any Lutz marbles in the bags. Almost any auctioneer can recognize a Lutz these days. And yes, some of the bags will be filled with slightly chipped, pale looking white latticinio center marbles of dubious ancestry. However, a few of the bags may contain small colorful gems as rare as any Lutz. Although overlooked by the "advanced collectors" these small marbles will appreciate as much in value as the large and unusual ones that they purchased earlier. A sharp kid with a loan from his dad can put down $30 to $40 for a bag of 10 to 20 marbles, pick out several excellent investment and collection grade specimens, and resell the remainder for what he paid for the group.

I have included in this book a plate of mixed small swirls (Plate 24) to emphasize how collectible they are. As we have already mentioned in some of the previous sections, some relatively simple color patterns were felt by the glassworkers to be too plain for large marbles. Thus some styles of small marbles are never even found in large marbles. Some of the marbles on Plate 24 are just there because they're attractive, however there are a number of types I'd like to point out as being particularly rare or collectible. The plate has more or less 12 rows which can be best distinguished on the left side.

I'll go through a brief guided tour from top to bottom. The top two rows show a variety of solid core marbles, many having a single color on a base color, a pattern unusual in large marbles. While the red on white and blue on white examples are attractive, the red on yellow and green on yellow examples (third and sixth from left top row) are particularly unusual and striking. Row three contains both small end-of-day or cloud marbles and what might best be called an expanded core mica. Such micas with either an expanded solid core (or a slightly shrunken onionskin, depending on your point of view) and a blizzard of mica in the outer glass, come primarily in small and medium sizes and are very rare in any size. Rows 3 and 4 on the right show a smattering of cores with translucent glass (more of these later). Row 4 on the left shows some deliberately made open core swirls and row 5 on the left shows what might best be termed expanded latticinio centers. These again are rare in small sizes and extremely rare in large sizes. Rows 5 through 8 on the right (row 6 is a single marble) are ribbon cores either twisted as in row 5, flat, or half twisted as in the following rows. The small ribbons are a truly beautiful and collectible marble.

Row 6 and the left of row 7 are a series of red and orange latticinio centers. As stated in the section on latticinio marbles, I have never seen a true red latticinio center in a large marble. Row 10 (left through center) shows a series of solid core marbles where the base color is something other than white or yellow. (The yellow marble shown is an unusual translucent color.) As discussed in the section on solid core marbles, those with cores of red or blue or green are extremely rare in any size.

Rows 9 and 10 on the right and row 11 center to right show more marbles in which translucent glass was used as part of a solid or divided core, including the translucent purple glass in the pair second from right in rows 10 and 11. Although translucent glass is sometimes used in large marbles as a border on the strands in a divided core or as an edge or border on the ridges in ridged solid core marbles, it is almost never used as an integral part of the core. Its use this way in small marbles (where the effect is attractive) is very limited. Small Joseph swirls are featured in row 11 (first, second, and fourth from left). Row 12 shows a few small onionskins, including a couple where the color remains as spots instead of lines. As explained in the section on onionskins, this would have to have been done intentionally, and would have required some effort on the part of the glassworker.

The listing just presented is not meant to be exhaustive, nor does it present all the potential sub-groups of small swirls which are rare or collectible. Hopefully, however, it will both stimulate more interest in smaller swirl marbles by advanced collectors and help new and young collectors realize that there are many more options available for those on a small budget than simply later machine made marbles. Remember that while some machine made marbles are unique, and will probably never be reproduced, other types could be remade easily if major marble companies got the "itch." Also the later machine made marbles, having been produced in more massive numbers and having been produced more recently, do not in my opinion have the appreciation potential of selectively purchased handmade swirls. Of course selective purchasing is the key in any case, whether buying handmade marbles or machine made marbles. It is the educated and selective collector whose collection will appreciate.

$\circ 6 \circ$
Individually Made Marbles

End-of-Day

End-of-day marbles resemble onionskins except that they have only a single pontil rod mark (Plate 25, lower group). Thus they were not cut from a cane but were made individually. The manufacturing process must have consisted of gathering a small amount of glass on the end of a rod and then covering it with a base color, perhaps by rolling it in powdered colored glass, reheating it in the furnace, and rolling it in the powdered glass again (see Chapter 4, Making of a Marble). After this the marble would be rolled over bits of crushed colored glass like the onionskins were. Further reheating and rolling would then fuse these pieces with the colored base, and additional clear glass would be added over the top. The crushed glass pieces would have to have been cooled to exactly the right temperature or the colors would have bled into the clear glass being put over the top of them. In some end-of-day marbles, as well as some onionskins, you can see wisps of color coming up into the clear from some of the pieces of crushed colored glass. This may have been done purposefully to create an effect, or it may be a sign of sloppy workmanship and the misjudging of temperature by the maker. In either case such bleeding of color does not allow these marbles to be called clouds. The term cloud is used for a completely different type of marble which will be discussed in the next section.

Because end-of-day marbles weren't pulled as were marbles cut from a cane, the crushed bits of color remain as spots rather than as lines. The mark of an end-of-day marble is that the color pattern forms sort of a balloon inside the clear glass, with the spots of color going right over the top of the pattern where the second pontil ought to be, instead of little lines forming which go toward the outer edge of the marble. Of course many of the larger onionskins also have spots of color, since those canes weren't pulled very much. A reasonable question would be, how do I know that my end-of-day marble isn't the end of a cane that produced a few large onionskins? The answer is, there may be no way to know. However, if the color pattern opens up completely at the top or seems to stop short in some sort of funny jagged pattern, then the chances are that it is an end-of-cane. After all, it stands to reason that someone producing an individual marble would take quite a bit of care to ensure that the color pattern was evenly distributed and consistent around the marble. On the other hand, it is also reasonable to expect that the colored portion might fail towards the end of a cane, which would result in the last marble having an open topped core of color. In financial terms it probably makes little difference, since both of these groups of marbles are extremely rare.

In fact, due to the rarity of this group of marbles, I am not presenting a table comparing the relative scarcity of different color patterns. After all, it would be hard to get a large enough sample size to differentiate between rare and very rare. End-of-days, like onionskins, come in both segmented and unsegmented color patterns. Examples of segmented end-of-days occur in the 3 o'clock and 6 o'clock positions in the lower circle of Plate 25. Of course, on an end-of-day, segmentation breaks down towards the top where all of the colors tend to merge. Other onionskin color patterns such as bicolored speckled (Plate 25, top right, lower circle) also occur. This marble also has mica flecks, a not too unusual addition to these already fairly labor intensive marbles. Since true end-of-days were only pulled slightly where they were cut from the pontil, all of the colored glass chunks remain as spots rather than lines. Thus the marble which has red spots on a yellow background (Plate 25, top left, lower circle) would probably have been a "single color" marble if pulled into a cane. Another variation worth looking for is demonstrated by the red and blue speckled marble (Plate 25, lower left of the circle). Notice that the red spots in this marble overlay the blue. Thus we have a triple layer of workmanship, with the artisan trying deliberately for an effect of translucent red floating over blue. As one might expect, small sized end-of-days are relatively rarer than the large sizes. If a glassmaker was going to spend the time and effort to produce an individual marble, and if it took about as much time and effort to produce a large marble as a small marble, then he might as well produce a large marble and get a little more money for it. I suspect that the smaller the marble, the higher the chances that it was really an end-of-cane rather than a true end-of-day.

Cloud and Paperweight

As stated before, cloud marbles are not end-of-days with bleeding colors or end-of-days in which the color pattern increases in diameter as it moves away from the pontil. Such variations are to be expected in handmade marbles, but they do not indicate any difference in the production technique. True cloud marbles, as pictured in my first edition, consist of bits of colored glass floating inside a clear glass sphere (Plate 25, center of upper row). In other words there is no base layer or solid coating around the marble as there is in the onionskin and end-of-day types. Instead there is an assortment of red, white, yellow, green, and blue pieces of glass randomly suspended within the marble. All of the colored chunks are either separate from one another or grouped in small bunches seeming to float here, there, and everywhere inside the sphere. To produce this marble would have taken a certain amount of time and energy. Since some of the colored glass pieces are clearly inside some of the others, the marble must have been made in multiple layers, clear with a coating of colored chips, another layer of clear, another layer of colored chips, and so on and so forth. Each of these batches of colored chips would have had to have been heated in an annealing oven before being applied to the surface of the marble. Thus two people would have been kept very busy for a long period of time, one heating the central mass with colored chips already on it, and the other going back and forth to retrieve trays of still more colored chips. It is no great surprise that such a labor intensive marble would be so rare.

One also finds marbles of this type in quite a small size, $\frac{5}{8}''$. On the one hand it seems unlikely that anyone would have taken the trouble to produce such a small marble by such a long involved painstaking method. On the other hand it seems unlikely that these would be end-of-the-cane, since again the small pieces of colored glass seem to float in the marble. I know of no method by which this could be produced accidentally, especially when the different colored chips are at different levels within the marble and are separate from one another. Therefore unless other proof arrives later, I'll keep classifying these as true cloud marbles.

Paperweight marbles, as the name implies, were made exactly like paper-weights. Their decoration is a series of rosettes or flowers which are made from an intricate grouping of colored canes. As was noted in the section on Nicholas Lutz, such patterns could be assembled ahead of time and then later inserted into the paperweight or marble as the case may be. To produce a marble with such a complex design would have taken both a skilled artisan and a fair amount of time. Such marbles (Plate 25, upper row, left and right) were made at the glass cottages in Thuringen, Germany. Correspondence from the German Toy Museum in Thuringen stated that marbles with inclusions were those with clay figures (sulphides) and those with "colorful glass flowers according to the Venetian Millefiori-technique." The paperweight design, with the glass flowers all facing one direction, can be enjoyed fully only when the marble is in one specific position. The use of such a design in a marble is self defeating. As the marble rolls or turns, the presentation of the design changes to a side view or a back view, neither of which is attractive. On the other hand a flat base like a paperweight would always position the design in the correct posture for the proper viewing. Therefore these marbles never worked well as a production item and are exceedingly rare, perhaps rarer than colored figures in sulphides.

Sulphides

Sulphide marbles are clear glass spheres containing white or silvery figures in the center. These marbles were made during the same time period and in the same area as the German swirls (i.e. in the province of Thuringen) starting about 1850 to 1860. Correspondence from the Museum for Glass Art in Lausche, Thuringen states that such marbles with inset animals, birds, or other motifs were produced in the village of Lausche by independent crafts people. This implies that the artisans making sulphide marbles may not have been associated with the cottage factories producing the cane-cut glass marbles. The same letter also states that "such handmade marbles were occasionally produced here even into the last post-war years." Although the translation is not entirely clear, the words "last post-war years" seem to imply that some sulphides may have been made into the late 1940s. Catalogs from the City Products Corporation still list sulphide marbles for sale in 1914 and presumably in 1915 (undated post-1914 City Products catalog). However sulphide marbles are not pictured or mentioned in the 1924–1926 editions of the Universal Toy Catalog put out by the German toy industry. Therefore large scale production of these marbles for export to other countries must have ceased either during World War I or shortly thereafter. The occasional production which might have occurred into the 1940s must have been on a very small scale.

Sulphide marbles have long been rumored to have been produced in England or the United States. Both production sites are possible or even probable. The Iowa City Flint Glass Manufacturing Company was reported to have produced sulphides during its less than 20 months of operation in 1880, 1881, and 1882. Sulphides containing a bust of James Garfield (president in 1881) may well have been made at that factory. A number of other American glass companies made decanters, water glasses, etc. which contained sulphide heads or other figures. Any of these factories might have produced some sulphide marbles. However catalogs from the Baltimore Bargain House, Butler Brothers, and City Products Corporation dating between 1910 and 1915 all clearly list sulphides under imported marbles. Thus at least the major merchandisers were not carrying sulphides from American companies during that period.

Of course imported could also mean marbles from England as well as Germany. Although we have no documentation that sulphide marbles were ever made in England this is at least a possibility, since the sulphide technique was pioneered by an Englishman named Pellatt (Charleston, 1984). He patented his "cameo encrustation" technique in 1819 under the name of "Crystallo-Ceramie." Pellatt prepared a white cameo from china clay and "super-silicate of potash" forming it in a mold and slightly firing it. Cameos were used in a variety of wares by the English, such as scent-flasks and spirit-decanters, but were primarily used for small decorative objects such as door handles and paperweights. The process used by Pellatt was not original, but was an improvement on foreign prototypes.

Figures for the sulphide marbles produced in Germany were made in the same way as the English cameos. China clay or kaolin (see Chapter Two) was pressed into a mold and dried slowly in a kiln at 25°C (Miller, 1966). The most common method for inserting the figure into the marble was to have one glass worker gather glass on the front of the rod and another press the figure into the soft glass. Glass from the edges of the ball could then be carefully folded over any portion of the figure remaining uncovered. The glass would have to be carefully smoothed down to eliminate bubbles. The marble was then probably rounded on a marver after which it was cut from the excess glass and rod using the marble scissors.

The silvery appearance of most of the figures in these marbles is caused by the refraction of the light through a microscopic air space between the surface of the glass and the surface of the figure. The figure had to have a porous surface in order to have good reflective properties. Both the glass and the figure had to be heated to the correct temperature before the figure was inserted into the glass. The figure could be fractured if the glass was too hot. If the figure was too hot it might expand and fracture the glass or it might lose much of its silvery luster. Bubbles were another major problem in sulphide marbles as most collectors know. Bubbles could be the result of a temperature missmatch between the figure and the glass. If the outer glass cooled more rapidly than the figure it might shrink away from the figure creating an opening. Bubbles could also develop if the figure was too porous or if smoke residue from the firing in the kiln remained in the figure.

Sulphides, like other marbles, were cooled by placing them in an annealing oven. Annealing ovens allow the marbles to cool slowly through time, keeping the glass from cracking. The larger the marble the longer it would have to be annealed and the more slowly it would have to be cooled. If the glass workers became impatient and removed the marble too soon, cracking would often occur. These marbles were probably fire polished by a final reheating.

Sulphide marbles were advertised in a variety of catalogs between 1895 and 1915. The earliest advertisers included Montgomery Ward and City Products. Later advertisers included City Products along with Our Traveler, Butler Brothers and William Croft and Sons. "Figured glass marbles" as they were usually called were almost always advertised in boxes of a dozen. The only original box of one dozen sulphides that I have ever seen is pictured in Fig. 6-1. This box is very unusual from a couple of aspects. First of all the marbles in it are quite small, measuring only $\frac{7}{8}''$. In all of the catalog advertisements that I have seen, the size range offered was from size 5 through size 10. Size 10 was approximately 2″ while size 5 was about $1\frac{3}{16}''$ in diameter. Thus the sulphides pictured in Fig. 6-1 are of a smaller size than any that I have ever seen advertised in a catalog. Also a few of the sulphides in this box have very small spots of red on them. Again these are the only sulphides in which I have seen this occur. This box came from an estate sale in Australia, and whether these particular marbles were produced in Germany or elsewhere is unknown. However they do give us a look at the way most children found their sulphide marbles when they unwrapped the gifts under the Christmas tree. Catalog prices would seem like real bargain basement rates today. William Croft and Sons, the Toronto retailer, sold the size 10 (2″) sulphides for $2 a dozen in 1912, while City Products would sell a dozen of the same size wholesale for only $ .84 as late as 1914.

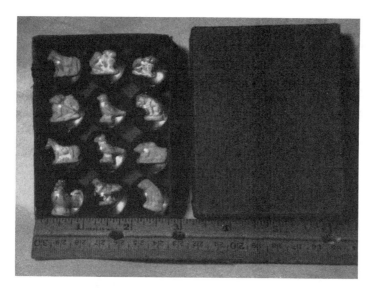

Fig. 6-1. A rare group of sulphides in their original box.

The most rare categories of sulphide marbles are those in which either the figure or the glass are colored, or in which two or more separate figures are present. All three of these conditions are extremely rare because, once again, none of them worked well as a production item. Colored glass sulphides (Plate 26) did not work well because figures became difficult to see unless the shade of color used in the glass was light, and the amount or depth of glass surrounding the figure was kept small. That is why many colored glass sulphides are small; the figures are not abnormally small, but the amount of glass surrounding the figure was kept to a minimum. This indicates that the German craftsmen realized the problem, and were trying to solve it. However in the end, figures worked best when they could be clearly seen. Notice how even the relatively light shade of blue in a fairly small marble (Plate 26, lower left) makes it difficult to see the figure of the dog inside. The pale blue works better with the elephant in the lower right, as does the green with the lion and eagle in the upper portion of the plate, and the amber surrounding the bear-like animal in the center. These are the three basic colors used for colored glass sulphides. I have never seen or heard of a sulphide figure encased in truly red glass. Occasionally one may see a figure in lavender or purple glass, and some sulphides may have been originally produced in that color. However the glass formula used in uncolored antique marbles can change to purple by exposure to sunlight, such as sitting on a window sill over a number of years. Therefore paying a premium for a sulphide in purple glass is always a little risky, especially if the color is pale.

As we have already seen, the refraction of light around the figure produces a silvery or reflective coating. If the figure is colored, the color is largely obscured by this coating. Thus coloring figures did not produce a satisfactory effect. The majority of colored animal figures resemble the dogs pictured in the upper right and bottom portions of Plate 27. The animals are usually spotted with a dark brown or black (it's hard to tell the difference) and are resting on a green base. This must have been a common color pattern for animals. I have seen a ram with black horns and eyes resting on a green base and a weasel and different breeds of dogs similarly colored. Even in this carefully shot photo it is difficult to see the color in some places due to the refraction of the light. Notice that the figures were not solidly colored, but that the color was used for accent. This is particularly true of the woman in the marble (Plate 27, upper left) where the hair and eyes are black and the neckline of the dress is dark blue. Colored numbers also occur in both blue and green as shown by the 5, 8, and 1 in the center of Plate 27. Such colored numbers are extremely rare, as are all sulphides with colored figures. Butler Brothers 1910 catalog lists both "figured glass" and "numeral glass" marbles under its imported marble subheading. The numeral glass marbles came only in size 7 ($1\frac{3}{8}''$ diameter) and were described as "large clear glass, silvered and green bronze numbers. Nos. 1 to 9 asstd." Thus green colored numbers were mixed in with regular silvered numbers in boxes of a dozen which were sold for $ .39 a box. A couple of those boxes would have turned out to be a pretty good investment!

Very rarely will there be a sulphide with three different colors on the figure. One of these, a spectacular rearing stallion with a golden mane, black eyes and hooves, on a green hill is pictured in Plate 28B. The yellow color used for the mane and tail is particularly unusual and the figure itself was done with greater detail and anatomical care than most. Other three- or four-color figures including peacocks and parrots are in the possession of lucky collectors. However at this point I feel I should issue a general warning against the purchase of sulphides with bright colors, such as bright yellows or greens. Colors used in the old figures included black, brown, blue, green, and amber. All of these generally had a dark or at least dull appearance. The amber on the horse's mane and tail shown in Plate 28B, is about the brightest color I have seen on an old figure. If you see a figure which is a flat chalky white rather than a silvery color, and which is decorated with bright yellows or greens rather than dull or dark shades, beware! Such a marble is almost certainly a reproduction, and I have seen these purchased by relatively advanced collectors for large sums of money. Remember that German glassworkers around the turn of the century would not have had the formulas or techniques to apply brilliant colors to sulphide figures; it would have been impossible for them to produce such a marble. After all, if such colors could have been used, the marbles would have been much more successful and would probably be less rare today. If you have any questions at all about the authenticity of a sulphide marble, contact someone who is an authority and get his opinion before you sink thousands of dollars into it.

Inserting two, much less three, separate figures into a marble would have been a task requiring considerable skill. First the glass would have been cooling constantly, so either the task had to be done quickly or the glass would require reheating, and reheating with a figure inside would probably have been nearly impossible without damaging the marble. Also the problem of leaving bubbles would have been compounded with multiple figures. In addition, a great deal of interior stress would have built up with multiple figures, and probably most marbles with multiple figures would have shattered sometime during the an- nealing process. Thus it is doubtful that these were ever produced in quantity, but were probably made as a demonstration of skill on the part of one of the master glassworkers. A good example of such skill is the sulphide with two fish figures passing each other in opposite directions (Fig. 6-2, center left). At least one marble with three separate figures is owned by a fortunate collector. Sometimes there is some confusion with the term "two subjects" or "two figures." Occasion- ally intricately designed figures such as the lovebirds or doves (Fig. 6-3, center left) or the man and woman and boy and girl at the top and upper left of Fig. 6-4 will be referred to as two figure sulphides. In reality these are elaborate sulphides depicting two individuals within a single molded figure. The term "two figures" or "two subjects" should best be left to those marbles having two separate figures in order to avoid confusion.

Sulphide marbles are often the first choice of new collectors because they are easily recognized and because it seems deceptively simple to understand compara- tive rarity within the group. In reality, understanding the relative rarity of different sulphide figures is exceedingly complex. I believe that the rarity of different sulphides is still poorly understood by the majority of collectors and that, as a result, collectors who take the time and trouble to educate themselves can still purchase very rare figures for the same price being paid for very common figures. What causes this complexity? Why is it that easily recognizable animals and figures haven't long ago been sorted into categories of common, unusual, and rare? Hasn't anyone ever asked collectors for a list of their sulphides, and then combined these into a table of relative rarity?

The overriding problem with determining rarity in sulphides comes in determining how to separate or lump figures. There is an amazing array of different figures which can be referred to as a single animal, say a horse or a dog. M.G. (Fred) Wright of Kokomo, Indiana was a collector who did a mail survey of sulphide marbles back in the 1960s when I was working on the first edition of this book. In a letter to me dated 12 May 1966, Fred stated that his data was "up to date for 1,034 sulphides." He also stated that "it would not be too hard to extend this information over another year and maybe pick up another 1,000 sulphides, bringing the list to over 2,000 sulphides." He then goes on to state: "I have perhaps seen and examined about 200 sulphides and have in my collection about 120. The amazing thing is that these objects are practically all different in detail though many may be similar in the general object that is being displayed, such as a standing squirrel with tail extending and holding a nut to his mouth. I have a

Fig. 6-2. Sulphide marbles—fish, reptiles, and amphibians.

Fig. 6-3. Sulphide marbles—wild birds.

Fig. 6-4. Sulphide
marbles—people.

number of such squirrels in my collection, all generally in the same on haunches position, but all different in detail."

Here Fred has accurately described one half of the problem that awaits classifiers of sulphide marbles. As can be seen in the table derived partly from Fred's data (Table 6-1) all dogs and all horses are not the same. But even this first cut using the position of the animal is not sufficient. Art Ward, an advanced sulphide collector from Atlanta, Georgia who is intelligent enough to know that all dogs are not alike, says he has 24 different varieties of that animal. When these different breeds are coupled with differences in position and other variations, such as having a collar or not, we suddenly find that the simple, cheap, readily

TABLE 6-1   RELATIVE RARITY OF SELECTED SULPHIDE FIGURES

Figure	#	Position	#
Dog	154	Standing	80
		Haunches	64
		Lying	10
Bear	86		
Lion	64		
Rabbit	53		
Horse	41	Rearing	16
		Grazing	11
		Standing	7
		Running	4
		Saddled	3
Elephant	25		
Fish	15		
Frog	9		
Swan	2		

available dog consists of a multitude of figures, some of which are common but some of which are exceedingly rare. Does this make a difference? Of course it does to a collector who realizes the potential for these marbles. I have in my collection duplicates of some marbles having children as the figure. These marbles would currently sell at many times the price for any given marble with a dog in it. Yet some figures of dogs may be far rarer than these particular figures of children. This is why the "simple" business of collecting sulphide marbles isn't simple at all!

The other half of the problem arises when the same figure is called by different names. This is very likely to happen when different individuals try to put a name on a sulphide, as is the case when different collectors send in a list of their figures. Suppose, as an example, we take a recent list of sulphide figures put together by the Marble Collectors Society of America from individual lists sent to them by collectors. The master list of figures contains all three of the following; crane, egret and stork (I'm surprised heron isn't on there too). Am I now to assume that these collectors are experts in avian taxonomy, or is there a possibility that some of these figures may indeed be the same bird? How about otters, weasels and ermine? Are they different? And what about horses and ponies? Grist (1988) identifies one horse-like figure as a pony and another as a horse, and then informs us that in the $1\frac{1}{4}''$ size the pony is only worth $\frac{2}{3}$ the price of a horse, while in the $2''$ size the pony is worth almost twice as much as the horse. Grist has properly acknowledged that the two horse-like figures are indeed different and that one of these may be rarer than the other, but it is doubtful that the German aritsan with his little clay mold in 1890 was thinking "pony" at the time. It is even more doubtful that anyone has the data right now to be able to accurately compare the rarity of such varying representations of the same animal, much less compare their rarity by size.

The only way to determine the rarity of the different sulphide figures would be for a single person to go from collection to collection, carrying along photos of marbles previously seen, and count each different figure, paying attention to all the details. Of course he would also have to count smaller collections and auctions in order not to bias his sample too much with advanced collections where duplicates may have been sold. To my knowledge such a compilation of sulphides has not been done. Unfortunately I have not had the time to do it for this book. (It will be on top of the list for my next edition.)

Of course this doesn't mean that some general statements can't be made. Certainly, figures of people, numbers, or angels are much rarer than figures of chickens, roosters, lambs, dogs, or bears. Table 6-1 gives a small view of some of the relative rarities. Others will be discussed plate by plate and can be deduced from the prices given in the price guide. Inanimate objects such as watches, cannons, drums and the like are extremely rare. (You will notice I don't have a plate of these.) In general my advice to new and old collectors alike is to pay more attention to detail. Visit other collectors, attend shows and keep a detailed list of the figures that you see. I repeat: collectors who take the time and trouble to educate themselves will be able to buy rare sulphides at discount prices. It is only a matter of time before either myself or someone else does the sort of survey that I have mentioned above. When such a survey is published, the well educated collectors who have done some sharp bargain hunting will see a tremendous appreciation in their collection.

So while we're all waiting around for the survey, let's take a casual stroll through the various types of sulphide figures. Cats, dogs, and horses (Fig. 6-5) are among the most popular figures in sulphide marbles. The dogs pictured (left column, top and center, and center column) show some of the variations available in both breed and postion. From the figures in Table 6-1, it appears that the normal four-footed pose is much more common than the lying pose (upper center), and that the begging pose (top left) is probably quite unusual. Similarly the running and sitting cat on the right, and the rearing and standing horse at the bottom demonstrate more variation in figures of the same kind of animal. While the rearing pose is really not that unusual in horses (Table 6-1) the horse on the left is unusual because it is wearing a saddle. Somehow during the dizzying photographic gyrations that went on for this book, one of my horses galloped over

Fig. 6-5. Sulphide marbles—dogs and cats.

into Fig. 6-6, where it can be seen rearing its head, so to speak, on the lower right. This figure and that of the horse in the lower right of Fig. 6-5 combine to prove a point mentioned earlier. Although both would be described by a collector as "rearing horses" the two figures are quite different. The horse in Fig. 6-5 is sculpted differently, including the carving of an open area under the horse's belly.

Fig. 6-6. Sulphide marbles—domestic animals.

One of these figures may, in fact, be much rarer than the other, although which is which I do not know.

Continuing on with Fig. 6-6 we get a look at other types of domestic animals. Again see how different the three sheep shown at the top of the plate are. One is grazing while the other two are standing with their head up. The sheep on the upper right has more detailed carving on the body to show the wool. In my opinion differences such as the wool detail indicate a different maker for the marble. Value is also added to marbles when figures show exceptional anatomical detail or carving. The goat at center left reaching over and biting its back, with an open area carved under its belly, shows this sort of detail. The pig at center middle and the cow at right center are representative of other barnyard animals pictured in sulphides. The two camels (lower left and bottom) are not identical—the bottom figure has a single hump while the figure to the left has two humps. These marbles indicate that at least some of the German craftsmen took care to distinguish between closely related species. In fact, sulphide figures seem to run the gamut from poorly detailed generalizations of animals, to superbly detailed animals which clearly represent a specific species or breed.

The start of our wild animal plates (Fig. 6-7) include some common (rabbits and squirrels) and some not so common (foxes and weasels) animals. Pictured are two different rabbits, (one sitting and one running) and two different squirrels to show the sort of variety that can be expected in these figures. The weasel or ermine (upper center) is obviously a member of that general family, although the species of animal cannot be identified with certainty. (I suggest to collectors that they buy such animals as weasels, and sell them as ermine or mink). In the center of the left column is a porcupine and in the center of the right column is a fox with an open area under its belly. Fig. 6-8 gets wilder yet with lions and elephants and bears (oh my!). The top three marbles show bears in three different positions. Certainly the "all fours" position (upper center) is much more common than either the "on haunches" position (upper left) or the standing position (upper right). The three lions in the lower part of Fig. 6-8 are in two different positions. However even the center and lower left lions are not identical—the position of the tail and detailing of the mane are quite different. Again one of these figures might be rarer than the other, and I have some confidence that eventually this will be known and published. Furthermore I am hopeful that eventually we might be able to connect certain specific figures with individual German makers. Also in Fig. 6-8 are an elephant (center left) and a wild boar (center right).

Barnyard fowl (Fig. 6-9) were also favorite figures in old sulphides. Roosters and chickens are relatively common. Ducks can be found either on their nest, as

Fig. 6-7. Sulphides—small wild animals.

Fig. 6-8. Sulphides—large wild animals.

in the example at the upper left, or off their nest. The goose (center left) could also be on a nest, but the neck up position and less nest-like detailing around the base make it possible that the goose is merely resting on the ground. It is just this sort of figure which could be described differently by two different collectors. While not a barnyard fowl, I needed something feathered and domestic to round out the photo, so I inserted the small parrot at lower right. Wild birds are found in Fig. 6-3. The owl at top left is unusual, as are the lovebirds below it (or facing doves if you prefer), and the vulture at lower right. The eagle at lower left is uncommon, as is the figure of a heron catching a fish (center). That latter figure shows a less frequent style of sulphide in which an animal is shown in relief on a solid block. In this particular figure the carving is good and the relief is adequate to demonstrate both the bird and the fish. In some cases the detail is poor on such figures, and what is being depicted is hard to decipher. The long tailed and short

109

Fig. 6-9. Sulphides—
domestic birds.

tailed birds at center and upper right of the photo would both be referred to as just
a bird by some collectors and would be called various names by others. I suspect
the bird at center right has been referred to as a partridge more than once, and this
may be as good a guess as any.

Our cold-blooded vertebrate plate (Fig. 6-2) is dominated by fish, the most
common figures in this group. Such things as frogs and the hard to see lizard on a
rock at the lower right are found less often. Although the three single fish look
very similar they are all somewhat different. The top two, however, are
stylistically very similar, particularly in the scaling, and differ only in the
characteristics of the head. The fish at center right has had the scales formed quite

differently. It is interesting to speculate about such similar figures with slightly different detailing. Perhaps these were just slightly different molds produced by the same individual. Perhaps some of the detailing was even added later, in which case these would just be variations expected in handmade objects and should be considered the same figure. Such subjective decisions on when to lump or split figures will eventually have to be made.

Fortunately I decided against combining the monkeys on Fig. 6-10 with the fish in the previous photo and referring to it as a "fish and chimps" plate. Chimps,

Fig. 6-10. Sulphides—monkeys.

monkeys, and other not quite human figures are depicted in a wide variety of styles. These range from the natural animal pose of the monkey in the upper right to the much more human-like sitting postures of the creatures at lower left and lower right. The lower left figure definitely looks like a chimpanzee, while the lower right figure is very strange in appearance although definitely not human. The figure at bottom also does not have a human face, and may either be standing or leaning slightly against a stump to his rear. The monkey in the top left marble is dressed in a hat, and the one at top not only has some clothing but is playing a drum. Such half-human figures playing instruments of various kinds are encountered once in a blue moon. I'm of the opinion that these were meant to be some sort of mythological creature—neither man nor animal.

Human figures come in two basic types, children and adults. That children are much more common than adults should come as no surprise since most of these marbles were sold to children. The children, both boys and girls, are depicted doing a wide variety of activities in all kinds of dress. The boy at center left of Fig. 6-11 wears a hat, is blowing a horn, and appears to be riding some sort of hobby horse. (Because of the horn this figure has been referred to as "little boy blue," although I don't know if that was the intent of its maker). Other active play figures are the boy (lower center) who is on his knees holding a small sailboat in his hands, and the girl at upper right in a rather formal outfit holding a croquet mallet and a croquet ball. The girl at right center is reading a book, and the girl at upper center is holding a doll on her lap, although the detail is not very sharp. The girl at lower left is sitting in a nicely detailed chair. Both the seated girl at upper left and the kneeling child at lower right are nude figures. The former has one hand on her breast and one hand on her head (bathing?), and the latter has both hands folded on the chest (praying?).

The couple in Fig. 6-4 (upper left) are also probably children rather than adults. The man and woman at the top of Fig. 6-4 are sharply detailed; the man having a musket and being superbly detailed in the back as well as the front. The man on the stump (upper right) and the formally dressed woman with the bubble (center) have quite a bit of detailing in their costumes, including rows of buttons which are not quite visible in the photo. Busts, like other human figures, are quite rare. The two at the bottom of the photo might be Jenny Lind and Beethoven, although one can never be sure unless the bust is labeled, as was done on some sulphides. These busts and busts of presidents indicate that such marbles may have been meant more for adults as memorabilia or as campaign items rather than as toys for children.

Fig. 6-11. Sulphides—children.

Religious figures rank with figures of adults as being quite scarce. Christ on the cross (Fig. 6-12, right) is a famous, if not very common, figure which has several variations. The angels at top center and bottom are nicely detailed on both front and back. The angel in the center has the finest detail of all. She is wearing a short tunic and her hands are folded in prayer. The angels on the top and bottom are depicted as being naked; the one at the top has her wings spread, and the one at the bottom is holding a small wreath in front of her pelvic area. Once again, these three sulphides would be counted as "angels" in a mail survey, even though the figures are really as different from each other as they are from the cupid head (or angel head and wings) at left. Incidentally it is interesting that such a high percentage of human figures were depicted as nude in marbles supposedly designed for children, and produced, at least in part, during the Victorian era, which we think of today as being straight-laced about such things.

Numbers (Fig. 6-13) are unusual and desirable figures in sulphide marbles. As mentioned previously, the 1910 Butler Brothers catalog advertised such "numeral glass marbles" for sale. They came only in a single size ($1\frac{3}{8}''$ or size 7), and thus might be expected to have a smaller size range than sulphides with animals in them. Also the advertisement stated that "numbers 1 to 9 asstd." were in each box. This means that numbers other than 1 to 9, such as the 10 depicted at upper left, would be very rare. Many of you will by now have noticed how different the 5 (center right) and the 8 (lower left) look as compared to the rest of

Fig. 6-13. Sulphides—numbers.

Fig. 6-12. Sulphides—religious figures.

the marbles in Fig. 6-13. This is because these two numbers are reproductions, probably made sometime in the 1960s. They can be distinguished by their squared off look, and by the flat white chalky appearance. They do not have the more silvery or bubbly appearance of the other marbles, indicating the use of a technique or glass type not available to the old German makers. While such marbles are now becoming collectible their value is no where near that of the old style numbers. Luckily these reproductions are fairly easy to spot, once you have seen one. Notice that the old freestyle marbles are more curvy, even to the point that the backwards 3 in the upper center is hard to tell from an 8. The 6 at lower right could well be a 9. The 10 and 6 at the top of the plate are on disks or coins, and such numbers are even rarer than the freestanding style.

$\circ 7 \circ$
Transition and Machine-Made Marbles

Nothing has been more exciting during the writing of this edition than the unfolding story of the first companies to use semi-automated or automated processes to produce glass marbles. This is truly an American story, since the original German industry did not switch to automation until 1926, at least 20 years after semi-automated machinery was being used in the United States. The unfolding tale of these companies has been and continues to be a giant detective story, with various marble enthusiasts running down one lead or another. Before I start talking about individual companies and types of marbles, I want to give you an overview of how this story developed. However, to keep this book from becoming a two or three volume set, I'll confine my discussions in this chapter to companies established before the end of the 1920s, and to marbles made no later than the 1930s. Since we now know that the hand-cut marbles made from canes were produced into the mid-1920s, they are no more "antique" than are the early machine-made marbles.

In my small section on "Modern Machine Marbles" in the first edition, I managed to name most of the major players: the Navarre Glass Marble and Specialty Company, M.F. Christensen, Akro Agate, and the Peltier Glass Company. In this edition I will also discuss one other company, the Christensen

Agate Company of Cambridge, Ohio. In the first edition I had Navarre producing handmade, cane cut marbles and had M.F. Christensen producing machine-made marbles by 1905. I also noted that Akro Agate was formed in 1911 and that a change in Akro Agate occurred in 1914. Randall and Webb (1988) have since published additional information on the American glass companies, their machinery, and the patents that were given for those machines. However, their book places the M.F. Christensen company in Steubenville, Ohio and fails to describe the type of marbles made either at M.F. Christensen or at Navarre. (My first edition did not give any location for the Christensen factory, and also failed to describe marbles from that company.)

At that point in time we were left with a lot of nagging questions. First of all, the 1910 Sears Roebuck and Company catalog listed a series of marbles called "national onyx." That same year the Butler Brothers catalog listed American onyx marbles and American cornelian marbles; moreover both of these are listed under a section entitled "American Marbles" as opposed to another section entitled "Imported Marbles." Also, imitation onyx marbles (for which there is no picture) are listed in a 1903 Our Traveler catalog. Even more troubling, the spring and summer Montgomery Ward catalog for 1899 listed two series of boxes containing marbles of different sizes under the heading American Glass Marbles. One was called "onyx style" and the other was called "assorted colors, glass."

The pictures in the 1910 catalogs look like machine produced marbles rather than hand-cut marbles, although catalog pictures fail to disclose whether the marbles had a single pontil or no pontil at all. If these were machine produced marbles, who was making them in enough quantity to sell through major retail outlets? Certainly not Peltier, they didn't start to make marbles until over 15 years later. Certainly not Akro Agate, they were established in 1911 and didn't start making their own marbles until 1914. Suddenly the M.F. Christensen company began to look more and more important. And what about the transition marbles? Were they really made by a transitional semi-automated method? Certainly they couldn't all be end-of-cane marbles! Could they have been, as suggested by Morrison and Terison, a way of disposing of scrap glass? Certainly not! Who would pay a worker good wages to sit around outside a factory making marbles out of scrap glass? Besides, enough of these marbles are still in existence to demonstrate that they were a production item, not something produced in someone's spare time. However such a production method would not have been able to compete with more fully automated machines that could produce perfectly spherical marbles. Thus transition marbles would have to have been made before automation improvements eliminated the pontil. That put us back to square one. When were the first non-pontil machine made marbles produced?

Into this quagmire of questions suddenly came a ray of light. In November of 1989 the Buckeye Marble Collectors Club received a letter from Michael Cohill, president of Group Ideate, Inc. Michael's letter stated that they were the manufacturers of "100% polymer, outdoor, active play toys," and that they had recently moved their manufacturing facilities to the home of M.F. Christensen and Sons of Akron, Ohio. The letter requested information on the M.F. Christensen and Son Toy Marble Company and mentioned that they had found memorabilia, sales information, and samples of the company's marbles at the site. This was exciting information, not only because of the discovery of the sales information, but also because it placed the M.F. Christensen Company in Akron rather than in Steubenville. On a mildly historic day in January of 1990 I drove up to Akron and met with Michael Cohill at the site of the old Christensen and Son Company. The information found there, along with a great deal of further research provided later by Michael Cohill (both personal communication and Cohill, 1990), will provide the backbone of the M.F. Christensen portion of this text as well as much of the Akro Agate section. However, suffice it to say that only 15 or 20 minutes of looking over the records were enough to convince me that M.F. Christensen was supplying large numbers of perfectly good, non-pontil, machine-made marbles to major retailers at least as early as 1907. Thus, logically, the company which produced the transition marbles must have been in operation before Christensen, probably prior to 1905. Now the Navarre Glass Marble and Specialty Company began to look more and more important.

Transition Marbles

THE NAVARRE GLASS MARBLE AND SPECIALTY COMPANY

On the drive back from Akron I thought over what I knew (or thought I knew, which wasn't much), about the glassworks at Navarre. I knew they had been in business for only a short time in the late 1890s. I also knew that a number of articles and newspaper reports claimed that the marbles made at Navarre were handmade, and in fact went so far as to describe swirled glass designs and sulphide animals. This picture of a short-lived factory making hand wrought glass marbles was at odds with the type of operation needed to supply Montgomery Ward with "onyx style" marbles in 1899. However I also remembered a conversation with another Ohio collector who had been to Navarre and visited the historical society there. I asked him if he had seen any marbles and he said that he had, but he hadn't been very impressed, they were just some "dark purple and greenish ones." It dawned on me months later that this is not the way an experienced marble collector would describe German swirl style marbles. So with rising excitement I went the next day to the library at Ohio State University, thumbed through their microfiche listing of telephone numbers for different cities in Ohio, and finally located a number for the mayor's office in the little village of Navarre. After several phone calls I was directed to Bill Deal, who invited me down to see the Navarre-Bethlehem Township Historical Society and their marble collection, even though it was in the middle of winter and things weren't officially open.

As soon as I saw the display case in the historical society I knew another piece of the puzzle had fallen into place. Certainly there were German swirl style marbles in the case, but alongside them and outnumbering them were marbles often referred to by collectors as slag. These slags were in fact the "onyx style" marbles produced by the Navarre Glass Marble and Specialty Company. Many of them resembled later types, having white swirled up through purple (Plate 29, left center), green (Plate 29, right center), or brown (Plate 29, bottom) inside the glass. Many in the case had the white swirled almost on the surface running up the side of the marble as a perfectly spiraled band. Bill then brought out a gallon of scrap glass that he had obtained from the owners of a house built on the old factory dump site. This jar was even more illuminating than the display in the case. The entire jar was filled with pieces and bits of slag or onyx glass. Nowhere were there any bits or fragments of latticinio canes or the other sorts of things one would find at a factory producing German swirl type marbles as a production item. Instead the jar was filled with purple and white, green and white, and brown and white pieces of glass (Plate 29) and very few pieces of red and white glass. Thus the basic imitation onyx glass formulas, including red and white, and the technique for gathering two different glass colors into a single marble had been used at Navarre prior to the opening of the M.F. Christensen Company in Akron, and much before the opening of the Akro Agate Company.

Nor was Bill's description of the plant one of a small operation. He talked about old photos of the village taken after construction of the factory, when the factory's smokestack obscured the view of one of the local churches. Before leaving town I followed Bill's directions down to the railroad tracks near the location of the factory's old dump site. After about twenty minutes of poking around I filled up a bag with pieces of slag glass, again mainly purple, with some green and some brown, and managed to scrape up one or two pieces that looked suspiciously like marbles gone bad (Plate 29). Again a dump site of the size described by Bill must have had its origins from a large factory producing over a number of years.

Unfortunately actual records regarding the operation at Navarre have not come to light, and the later reports written about the company are conflicting. A motley assortment of references, including a couple of newspaper articles (Navarre), agree that the company failed in 1901. The articles tend to disagree about when the company opened, or more precisely, they fail to mention when the company opened. A couple of the articles mention that the company was making marbles in 1897. A couple other articles mention that Emile Converse was president and superintendent of the plant from 1896 to 1901. This would imply that the plant was founded in 1896 and began production in 1897, although the plant could have been producing marbles earlier under another president or superintendent. Nevertheless the transition marbles were probably produced within the 1896 to 1901 time period. The size of the factory and the style of marbles being produced make it almost certain that the "onyx style" marbles listed in the 1899 Montgomery Ward catalog were from Navarre.

The company was also credited with making glass balls for the feet of piano stools and tables, paperweights, glass canes, and hatpins with marbles at the tip. The latter apparently were a major production item and are described in one of the newspaper articles (Fisher, 1975) as follows: "The hatpins were made with a small marble on the head. This was made attractive by using black glass and through the skill of the operator, a fine spiral of white glass was curled around it." In other words the hatpins were in the style of the transition marbles. The same article also mentions that children passing by the factory routinely yelled for marbles to be thrown out by those working inside. Apparently the workers usually obliged, although occasionally some joker would throw out a hot one to watch some poor unfortunate lad yelp and hop around for a while.

The closing of the plant brings an even more bewildering display of conflicting stories. Most articles agree that the plant failed because it was unable, in the end, to compete with the imported marbles from Germany. A couple articles mention that the owners (really J.H. Leighton) moved to Steubenville, Ohio to continue to make marbles until 1902 when the plant failed again. Note that this second company in Steubenville would have been in operation for only a year. A couple articles mention that while Emile Converse was president of the company or companies, a George Leighton of Akron held the patent rights. Randall and Webb (1988) list a patent granted in July of 1903 for "a tool for making marbles" to Jeremiah J. Leiter of Canton, Ohio assigned to Emile P. Converse of Massillon, Ohio. However the date of this patent would seemed to be after the collapse of the second factory and well after the operation at Navarre. Were Leiter and Converse simply patenting, after the fact, a tool that had been in use at Navarre and Steubenville?

Apparently, Jeremiah Leiter, George Leighton, and J.H. Leighton may all have been the same individual. James Harvey Leighton, you may recall, first appeared on the marble scene as the superintendent for the Iowa City Flint Glass Manufacturing Company. From there he touched all the bases, doing stints in Ottawa, Illinois and Akron, Ohio; running the Navarre factory; and then going on to Steubenville (Cohill, personal communication). In Akron he had an agreement with Samuel Dyke to produce glass marbles along with the clay ones already being made at the American Marble and Toy Manufacturing Company. In fact, Leighton was involved with several short-lived glass marble "factories" in and around Akron. Leighton was a glass master with a large color palette (estimated at 22 shades by Cohill, 1990), who invented many of the onyx (slag) colors (or at least color combinations), perhaps including the famous oxblood. He also may well have pioneered the gathering technique used to make the new transition marbles directly instead of first producing glass canes, thus greatly reducing the labor involved.

What about M.F. Christensen's connection (if any) with Navarre? Fisher (1975) states: "M.L. Christensen Co. of Akron attempted to operate the Navarre plant after Converse gave up the project but was unable to make it show a profit." Although Fisher mangled Christensen's name he at least placed his company correctly in Akron. Another article states that some of the Navarre workers were later hired by Christensen, who with his son, organized the company in 1901. Mike Cohill (1990) has discovered that Christensen hired Leighton to teach him how to make glass, and purchased his glass formulas from Leighton. Leighton worked with Christensen during the fall-winter of 1901–1902, or immediately after the Navarre Company closed. Thus the onyx style or slag marbles produced by Christensen were made with basically the same glass formula and gathering techniques used at Navarre, although, of course, the Christensen machinery for forming the marbles was quite different. Not only that, but Christensen's use of the term onyx for his own marbles seems to be taken directly from Navarre. Also,

Christensen later hired Harry Heinzelman, a former employee of the Navarre Glass Marble and Specialty Company, as his glass master for the M.F. Christensen & Son Company (Cohill, 1990). Thus Christensen was familiar with the operation at Navarre. Whether he was actually a part of the management towards the end or not is unknown at this time.

What do the transition marbles themselves tell us? First of all there is a wide variety of types which are dark purple, green, or brown glass with swirls of white (Plate 29). The pontil on these is cut in the fashion of the old German swirls. However they were formed by a different process, not by being cut from a cane or two pontils would be present. They were gathered individually but still hand cut one at a time by a workman, perhaps with "Jeremiah Leiter's tool for making marbles." This process is detailed in the Akro Agate section of this chapter. These "Navarre type" transitions may have been made elsewhere besides at Navarre, but certainly Navarre produced the bulk of them, being able to supply major retailers in the late 1890s.

However other types of transition marbles also exist. The gray and white and gray, white, and blue ones pictured on Plate 29 (center) are different color patterns than any found in the Navarre Historical Society dump site, although their pontil marks look similar. The group of clear blue and green glass with white swirls on Plate 29 (upper right) and the group of translucent "game marbles" (Plate 29, upper left) have quite different pontil marks from the Navarre style. The single pontil on these marbles has been ground. Not just a single ground surface but several facets appear at the site where the marble was cut. These facets are not rough, but are polished enough to give the illusion of looking into a series of tiny angled mirrors. Thus these two groups of "faceted transitions," the translucent game marbles and the swirled white within the transparent green, blue, and clear glass (Plate 29, upper third), were in all probability produced at the same factory. Again remember that companies producing any type of transition marbles must have operated in the very last part of the 1800s or the first five to eight years of the 1900s. They could not have survived competition with the likes of Christensen and Akro, and certainly neither Christensen nor Akro Agate were dumb enough to pay someone to sit around and make single marbles when they had machines producing tens of thousands. These faceted transitions, like the Navarre transitions, are rare. Their rarity is due to the narrow time frame between the first attempts at semi-automation and the success of Christensen in producing a completely spherical marble with no pontil. Perhaps the faceted transition marbles or the gray ones were produced at Steubenville, or perhaps they were produced at another factory about which we have no information at present.

Machine-Made Marbles

M.F. CHRISTENSEN AND SON COMPANY

Martin F. Christensen was born in Denmark in 1849 and immigrated to the United States in 1867 when he was 18 years old (Cohill, 1990). He first worked in the drop forge steel industry making tools and knives. Christensen was an inventor, and over the next thirty years he acquired a large number of patents on everything from the garden hoe to ball bearings. It was his patents on the production of ball bearings which established his personal fortune, and which apparently led to a life-long fascination for sphere machines. In 1900 Christensen purchased a block of land in the town of Akron, Ohio. By 1901 he had formed the M.F. Christensen and Son Company with his son Charles who was born in 1880 and would have been about 21 at the time. He applied in December of 1902 for his first marble machine patent. Randall and Webb (1988) described this machine as utilizing a pair of wheels with semi-circular grooves which moved in opposite directions and could only accommodate one marble at a time. However, in 1905 Christensen submitted an improved design which was considered significant enough by the patent office to be given a grounded patent, i.e. one with wider protection rights (Cohill, personal communication). The change itself was quite simple—he made one wheel larger than the other. This forced the piece of glass turning between the two wheels to rotate on a constantly changing axis, improving the rounding process. While one can speculate that some transition type marbles may have been made by Christensen in the 1901 or 1902 experimental period before the first machine was patented, certainly the marbles found at the factory site are perfect spheres with no pontils.

An amazing array of original information was still present when Mike Cohill arrived in 1989, both at the factory site and in the house where Christensen's son Charles used to live. Among these items was a diary kept by Christensen himself in which were listed formulas for his various marbles and assorted sales information. The names and pictures of the marbles in this diary are immediately familiar to those who have looked at early catalogs. There are national onyx marbles, the same name and picture given in the Butler Brothers and Sears Roebuck and Co.

Fig. 7-1. An early ad for M.F. Christensen & Son Company, which produced a variety of marbles and glass balls.

catalogs in 1910. A little further down Christensen's list we come to American cornelian marbles, exactly the same title given in the Butler Brothers 1910 catalog. Furthermore Christensen sales material is replete with names that appear in Sears Roebuck and other catalogs; oriental jade marbles, Persian turquoise marbles, imperial jade marbles, moss agate or blood agate, and a variety of the onyx types. Not only that, but Christensen's diary and other documents detail sales of large numbers of marbles to such retailers as Montgomery Ward, Woolworth's, Sears, and Milton Bradley.

This was definitely not the sort of early glass works operation people tend to envision, with a few old duffers sitting around quaffing beers and turning out a few hundred marbles a day. During peak production (circa 1914) M.F. Christensen and Son turned out 2.3 million cornelian marbles during a two-month period (Cohill, 1990). These were also their most expensive marbles, being followed by oriental jade and Persian turquoise. These latter marbles were a single color, usually referred to as "game type" marbles. Although they are not illustrated in this book, I understand from Mike Cohill that they are identifiable from other types of game-style marbles (Cohill, 1990). If so, these should appreciate rapidly in value.

Christensen's brochures show that they made sizes 0 through 10, the latter would have been about 2″ in diameter. They also made glass balls for a variety of other purposes, as did Navarre. Among those listed by Christensen are glass balls used for ballot balls, furniture casters, pump valves, graining lithographic plates, and bottle stoppers.

Christensen sold almost all of his marbles wholesale to jobbers, retailers, and distributors. The 1910 prices on his American carnelian marbles were $7.70 per 1,000 for size 0 up to $11 per 1,000 for size 4. Size 4 national onyx marbles from the same year were selling for $6.70 per 1,000. Depending on their size, these marbles were packed in square or rectangular boxes containing 25 to 100 marbles each, or in a tapered salesman's sample box containing 9 marbles of varying sizes grading from small to large. Christensen only produced the onyx or slag type marbles in three colors; blue, green, and amber, with the amber appearing more brown than yellow. Slag marbles produced at M.F. Christensen are similar to those produced later by Akro Agate and others (Plate 30, bottom). All told, M.F. Christensen and Son only made 7 different types of marbles, a small amount of variety for such a large factory. This is probably partly due to the fact that M.F. Christensen himself was more interested in the marble making machinery than in the glass formulas, although he did do some limited experimentation beyond the glass formulas purchased from J.H. Leighton. This focus can also be seen by the fact that he did not retail any of the marbles but sold them to jobbers and distributors.

A number of the formulas used for the glass are listed in Christensen's diary. Several of these date from around 1910, when the formulas may have been revised. Arsenic, mentioned before as being used in some of the German marbles, was also used in some of Christensen's, including the opal marbles and the turquoise marbles. Other interesting ingredients for different marbles included manganese, brass oxide, and a couple forms of copper. The boxes he packed his marbles in were ordered from the B.F. Goodrich Co., who at this time owned a straw-board box company. Christensen also ordered barrels to store his marbles in from Jacob Lapp. These were seconds of sugar barrels (with hoops) which came in 30 cent and 35 cent varieties. Christensen also had to hire a drayman who, with his wagon and horse team, would cart the marbles off to the local railhead. The cost for this (with two men furnished) was 35 cents for 1 pound to 1,000 pounds and 75 cents for 1,000 pounds to a full load. However an extra 25 cents was given if a part of a load required an extra trip.

As I have mentioned, Christensen hired Harry Heinzelman, a former employee of the Navarre factory along with the Baughman family, also from Navarre (Cohill, 1990). He tried to get experienced people, and he showed by his management style, typical for that time period, that he wanted to retain his best workmen. While the workmen were paid fair wages for the times (50 cents per thousand marbles), Christensen also often gave them a down payment on the construction of their house, which of course was located on land that he owned. Besides, he would usually employ everyone in the family. The Baughman family (perhaps distant relatives) had seven members working at the factory. They ranged from the smallest child, who worked in packaging, to the mother who was an office clerk, to the aging father who was used as a day watchman. Glass workers in the 1800s and early 1900s were a fairly close knit group. As was the case with Christensen, glassworks tended to operate with a small group of families with all the members joining in the work.

This going concern probably largely came to an end because M.F. Christensen himself did; in October of 1915 he keeled over dead at the dinner table. The company continued for two more years into December of 1917, being run by M.F.'s son Charles. Then in 1917 a particularly cold December exhausted the gas supply in Akron, already low because of the war effort. In order to conserve gas for residences, all of the factories in the town were forced to close. For whatever reason, the Christensen and Son Co. never reopened. The remaining supply of marbles was bought by Akro Agate in 1918. Apparently dramatic deaths run in the Christensen family because Charles later dropped dead at Christmas dinner in 1922. The production of American marbles now shifted to Akro Agate which was itself a spin-off of the M.F. Christensen Co.

Marbles found at the Christensen factory often have small grooves in the surface, a by-product of the still primitive machine used at the company. These and other characteristics might be useful in separating marbles produced by Christensen from those produced by Akro Agate and other companies. However at this time such identifications are not certain and are hard to depict in a book of this nature. My best advice to collectors wishing to purchase early onyx or slag style marbles is to visit an advanced collector who already owns some and try to pick up the finer points of differentiating one company from another.

AKRO AGATE COMPANY

The Akro Agate story begins at the M.F. Christensen and Son Co. with Christensen's bookkeeper Horace C. Hill. Together with George T. Rankin and Gilbert C. Marsh, they came up with an idea to repackage and resell Christensen marbles (Cohill, 1990). The partners (Hill may have been a partner from the start or may have joined in 1912) named their new company the Akro Agate Co. The name (derived from the city of Akron) and trademark (a crow flying through a large letter A and holding marbles with its beak and feet) was applied for in March of 1911 and registered on August 22, 1911 (Randall and Webb, 1988). Meanwhile Hill was also trying to patent a marble machine based largely on plans stolen from Christensen (Cohill, 1990). Unfortunately, the marble industry also has its share of rogues and wheeler-dealers. Hill's first patent attempt in 1912 was rejected for being too similar to Christensen's patent, but the partners shrewdly made money by exploiting one of Martin Christensen's weaknesses. Christensen, with his background as an inventor and his real love being the design of sphere machines, never expended any effort to retail his own marbles. He was content to sell his marbles wholesale to jobbers and distributors who then took a second profit before the five and dime stores and others sold them to children and took a third profit. Apparently this wholesale distribution produced enough profit for Christensen, but it also made an opening for Akro.

Marsh, Rankin and Hill decided to package Christensen's marbles under their own Akro trademark (Randall and Webb, 1988). They set up shop in the Marsh and Wagner shoe store in Akron, which (as we now know) was conveniently close to the Christensen factory. They then purchased marbles wholesale from Christensen, packaged them in cellophane bags, and sold these packages to retail outlets. These small bags, many containing only five marbles, turned out to be a huge marketing success at a time when marbles ordinarily had to be purchased in lots of 25 to 100 depending upon the size of the box. Thus for at least the first three years of its existence, Akro Agate made all its money by marketing marbles under their trademark that were actually produced at the M.F. Christensen factory.

It is difficult to understand why M.F. Christensen, who almost certainly knew of Hill's attempts to patent a machine very similar to his own, and who now suspected Hill of embezzlement, would have cheerfully supplied so many marbles to this upstart rival company. However, the last recorded sales to Akro were in February 1912, although Akro Agate continued to sell Christensen agates for two more years (Cohill, 1990). This is probably due to some more of Hill's creative bookkeeping. Hill quit the M.F. Christensen and Son Company in August 1913.

In 1914 Horace Hill and Akro Agate moved to Clarksburg, West Virginia, where cheap natural gas and a good supply of silica sand were both available. Akro's machine began producing marbles late in 1914, although the Akro Agate Co. may still have been selling some of Christensen's marbles at this time. Hill's resubmitted patent was finally granted in December of 1915. His machine was similar to Christensen's except that it replaced the two wheels with two sets of cylinders having helical grooves. The wheels of Christensen's machine could only hold one marble at a time and that marble had to be spun until it was cool enough to be dropped into an annealing bucket.

The advantage of Hill's machine was that the marbles cooled as they went down the length of the rollers, so that one marble after another could start traveling along the path. Also the rollers were designed to allow the marbles to drop off automatically when they reached the end, as opposed to the Christensen wheels which had to be levered apart by a workman (Randall and Webb, 1988). Hill's machine produced twice the number of marbles in the same amount of time as did Christensen's machine. However there was also a trade-off; Hill's machine had lost the rounding advantage that Christensen had gained in 1905 by making one wheel larger than the other (Cohill, 1990). This design problem caused Akro Agate to reject almost 20% of the marbles their machines produced. This large percentage of rejects at least partially neutralized the gain in speed of production. Nevertheless, by the end of their first fiscal year in June of 1915, Akro Agate had sold approximately 2 million marbles, establishing them as a major producer along with Christensen.

By this time Hill's past had caught up with him. M.F. Christensen had amassed enough evidence of Hill's embezzling while employed at the M.F. Christensen and Son Co. to take him to court. In March of 1915 Hill was convicted of embezzlement and sentenced to nine years in prison plus restitution. The prison sentence was waived, in order to aid Hill in repaying the money he had stolen. Apparently he had been fairly efficient, managing to steal about four thousand dollars, which in 1915 was a great deal of money. To the benefit of Akro, Hill also managed to steal most of the glass formulas and all of the addresses of Christensen's accounts. Christensen at the time was selling all over the world including such places as India and Malaysia (Cohill, 1990). Having these account addresses put Akro in a much better position than would be usual for a new marble company in its first few years. Of course one can also do some speculation about the origins of the design for Hill's marble machine. Christensen was known to work on new inventions for a long period of time, perfecting them before he submitted them for a patent. In any event Horace Hill died in the spring of 1916, one year after his conviction, and six months after the death of M.F. Christensen.

At this time Akro Agate was not yet financially stable; however Akro hired George A. Pflueger that same year. Pflueger was an expert at marketing and promoting and greatly helped the company's financial picture. Akro probably realized quite a bit of profit from their repackaging and sale of the Christensen stock (undoubtedly bought at a cheap price in 1918). Once again this demonstrates the difficulty of telling which company made which marble. In 1918 and 1919, as in 1911 through 1914, marbles sold in Akro Agate packages had actually been produced at the Christensen factory.

In February of 1919 Akro Agate hired John F. Early from Akron, Ohio as their plant superintendent (Randall and Webb, 1988). Early proved to be a competent inventor who through the years added a lot of improvements to Akro's machines. Early's first innovation was a major one: He offset the alignment of the grooved cylinders in Hill's machine. With the helical grooves in the two cylinders offset from each other, the marble now spun on a constantly changing axis. This design change was initiated in 1924, although a patent was not granted for it until 1930. Thus in 1924 Akro Agate finally regained the precision in rounding (by offsetting its cylinders) that Christensen had originally gained by making one wheel larger than the other about twenty years earlier.

So far in our discussion of marble machines we have talked only of the machinery used to round the marbles and not the process of obtaining the molten or "plastic stage" glob of glass to begin with. Up until the late 1920s, the actual glass to be rounded was supplied by "gathering boys" (really adults) who manually took hot glass from the furnace with a metal rod (Randall and Webb, 1988). J.H. Leighton may have pioneered this technique which was a great advance over the need to construct canes, at least as far as speed of production was concerned. First molten glass was ladled from the main melting pot into a smaller pot for the gathering boy to work. The two color onyx designs were made by first ladling in the color for the main body of the marble and then ladling in the color for the striping. Different colors or types of glass have different densities and if this operation was done carefully one color would float on top of the other. The skill of the gathering boy would then come into play as he dipped the preheated head of the rod or punty into the two glass layers, causing glass of both colors to adhere to the rod. It was the gathering boy's skill at inserting the rod and twisting the punty which resulted in the swirls within the marble. When the rod was withdrawn from the pot, a cutoff man would shear a portion of the glass off which would then start spinning on one of the marble machines.

This gathering then remained largely unchanged while the advances came in the ability to round the marbles after they were cut off the punty. Automatic feeders which eliminated the gathering boys were first invented by Ira Freese and used by Akro Agate in 1925 (Randall and Webb, 1988). Such feeders were later improved by John F. Early and Clinton F. Israel (who began working for Akro Agate in 1926). These improvements in feeding the glass to the rounding machines not only gave consistent and uniform patterns (like corkscrews), but eventually allowed for three color rather than just two color marbles.

In 1928 Early applied for another patent which consisted of a double set of cylinders and a dual feeding mechanism. This "duplex machine" more than doubled the production of each machine. By 1929 the Akro Agate company was at the peak of its career, at least as far as marbles were concerned. Although the company would continue to produce marbles until 1950, the loss of a number of crucial employees in 1930 (including John F. Early and Clinton F. Israel) was a serious blow. Early, Israel, and others joined forces to form the Master Marble Company later in 1930. That company and others formed in the 30s, 40s, and 50s will not be discussed in this book, although some of the marbles they produced are now collectible.

Akro Agate produced a variety of marbles during the 1920s and into the early 1930s. Their salesman sample box at the lower right of Plate 31 is interesting since it gives the original names of a variety of their marbles. While the royals had a patch of color, the onyx, prize name, tricolor, and ace varieties were all types of corkscrews. Corkscrews are also featured at the lower right of Plate 30 and were only produced by the Akro Agate Co. At the lower left of Plate 30 are a variety of corkscrew with white and clear which is referred to by collectors as Popeyes. Presumably this is because these marbles were the ones featured in boxes with a picture of Popeye the Sailor on the cover. Just above the Popeyes in Plate 30 are marbles referred to as limeade and lemonade, in reality another type of corkscrew. Continuing around the outer circle on Plate 30 above the lemonade we have three metallics or marbles containing some gray metallic looking areas. The manufacturers of both the latter marbles and the next group, those having aventurine glass (often green) are unknown. Next come a series of marbles having a dark red glass referred to as oxblood. These marbles are generally presumed to have been made by Akro Agate, although this cannot be said with complete certainty. At upper left continuing around Plate 30 are lemonade oxbloods followed to their right by silver onyx or silver oxbloods, and then right again to golden onyx or egg yolk oxbloods. Blue onyx or blue oxbloods come next followed by a group of bricks, marbles made completely of the dark red oxblood color. The next two groups may be somewhat later (1930s) and their company of manufacture is more open to question. These include at center right a large group of multi-color opaque swirls, and below them two bumblebees and a cub scout.

Corkscrews were probably the first marbles to be made using the new glass feeding machinery invented by John F. Early. They and later marbles with more controlled or repeatable color patterns, like the multi-colored opaque swirls, cub scouts, and bumblebees were all turned out by machinery very similar to that still in use today. Unfortunately that makes these types more vulnerable to mass reproduction than many of the other marbles discussed in this book. However Akro also produced a large number of the imitation onyx or slag type of marble in the 1920s, such as those depicted in the box at the bottom center of Plate 31.

Perhaps this is a good place to note that I took the cardinal reds located in the center of the latter box and second from right in the Akro saleman's box and compared them to red imitation onyx marbles from both the Christensen box at top center and from another Christensen box not pictured. The result, after a fairly lengthy and detailed examination, was that I was unable to tell the Akro marbles from the Christensen marbles. Had I mixed them together I doubt seriously that I or any other self-proclaimed expert could have correctly sorted them out again. Other color patterns of imitation onyx are also very similar, both in the actual color and in the pattern of white swirled through it. In other words, the variation within a given box from a given company is as great or greater than the variation between companies. Since this is the case, I have serious doubts that loose, unboxed marbles of this variety can ever be assigned to a particular company with any amount of accuracy, unless it is known that only one of the companies used a particular color.

THE CHRISTENSEN AGATE COMPANY

The last of the Ohio marble companies which came into production before the 1930s, and about which I have good information, is the Christensen Agate Co. located in Cambridge, Ohio. Although the name of this company is obviously derived from the M.F. Christensen and Son Co. founded in Akron at the turn of the century, both M.F. Christensen and his son Charles died prior to the incorporation of this company in Akron in 1925. The Akron businessmen who formed the company, W.F. Jones, H.H. Cupler, Owen M. Roderick, Robert C. Ryder, and Beulah P. Hartman were not related to M.F. Christensen nor were they part of his original company as far as is known (Carskadden and Randall, 1987). Apparently the Christensen name was used because it was still recognizable to retailers as having been a sizable producer of marbles in Ohio. One of the key people in the company was Howard M. Jenkins, originally of Pittsburgh, who was the company president and held the patents for its marble machines. Jenkins was granted a patent in 1924 for a machine that was similar to Horace Hill's (Randall and Webb, 1988). Jenkins' machine had eight different pairs of grooved wheels and could be adjusted to make marbles of different sizes. While such a machine was not a great technological advance, it was certainly efficient and productive for the period. Jenkins apparently ran the company from the start, the first factory being established in Payne, Ohio. The company operated in Payne for part of 1925 through 1927.

In 1927 operations were moved to Cambridge, Ohio, where the new factory was established in a small brick building next to the Cambridge Glass Co., and on the old B. & O. Railroad. The plant operated in Cambridge from 1927 to 1931, when actual production of marbles ceased. The company's charter was finally cancelled in 1933 for failure to pay franchise tax. Virtually nothing is known of the types of marbles produced at the Christensen Agate Co. during its existence in Payne. On the other hand a wide variety of unique and beautiful marbles, already much in demand by collectors, were produced by this same company while in Cambridge. The reason for this difference is not so much that the plant was in operation longer in Cambridge, but rather because of another remarkable individual that joined the company at that time. Arnold Fiedler had learned his glassworking art in Germany, where he had been employed for a time in the glass marble industry. He came to the U.S. with a variety of European glass working secrets. He also came with an extremely sophisticated color sense and the ability to put it to use. He was able to produce dozens of colors not available to other marble companies of the era. These colors, combined with innovative ways of mixing them or adding them to a base, produced some truly unique and spectacular marbles (Plates 30 and 31).

Fiedler had been working at the Cambridge Glass Co. while Christensen Agate was playing out its unspectacular stay in Payne. Fielder, in fact, may have been the reason that the entire company was moved to Cambridge. An article in

Crockery and Glass Journal from November of 1927 stated that the new Cambridge factory had a goal to produce 300,000 marbles a day "in a short time." The company undoubtedly obtained this goal, not only producing the imitation onyx style marbles which had been pioneered at Navarre and at M.F. Christensen but also producing such exotic varieties as "flames" (Plate 30, lower center), and "guineas" (Plate 30, center left), and a marble similar to a guinea but with the guinea colors swirled in clear glass (Plate 30, center right). These latter marbles have been called cyclones by some collectors. That these marbles were actually produced at the Cambridge factory has been verified, not only by the existence of original marked boxes (Plate 31, upper left) but also by the shards and misshapen marbles of these same types which have been found in the dump behind the factory site.

Some marble boxes from the Christensen Agate Co. list the Gropper Onyx Marble Co. of New York as "sales distributors"; Gropper also functioned as a middle man for the Peltier Glass Factory in Ottawa, Illinois and others. Most of the boxes, however, simply have The Christensen Agate Company, Cambridge, Ohio and some have the words "World's Best Toy Marbles" (Plate 31, top row). Perhaps this is a good place to mention that the spectacular box of guineas featured at the top left of Plate 31 was purportedly the first such box to be packed when guinea marbles went into production. The box was presented to veteran packer Thelma Poorman by the company owners in appreciation of her good work. Since she probably packed the box herself, it is no wonder that all the marbles are so nice. The other two Christensen boxes contain the imitation onyx or slag marbles so commonly produced during the 1920s, except for the center row of the American Agate Box which features some flames.

I have no information on why the Cambridge plant closed when it did. Whatever happened, Arnold Fiedler's innovative glass working techniques were never passed on to other glass workers. Apparently Arnold kept his old world secrets to himself alone, not even sharing them with other members of his family. He quite literally took them to his grave. On the other hand Mr. Fiedler could be a very caring and compassionate sort. Elliott Pattison was Mr. Fiedler's chauffeur when he was only 14 or 15 years old. He recalls Mr. Fiedler visiting him in the hospital when he was sick with appendicitis and bringing him a 25 pound sugar sack full of marbles (Carskadden and Randall, 1987). However, giving away marbles may have been easier than giving away secret technology. The result of Mr. Fiedler's refusal to train a younger generation is that we have, for a brief time period in the late 1920s, a marble factory producing some spectacular and unique collectible types, and then vanishing from the scene. Nothing quite like the Christensen Agate Co. in Cambridge would ever be seen again.

THE PELTIER GLASS COMPANY

While all this activity was going on in Ohio, what was happening in Illinois? Actually quite a bit was going on in the glass industry, particularly in the small town of Ottawa, Illinois on the banks of the Illinois River. Ottawa happened to be situated near the richest vein of silica sand in the United States. This sand was 99.9% pure silica; obviously an enticement to the glass industry in which silica was the main ingredient. In 1867 the first glass factory west of Pittsburgh was started in Ottawa by Catlin and Caton. Only five years later the Bottle and Flint Glass Co. was employing 160 men, and the glass industry in Ottawa was underway. In 1886 Victor Peltier arrived from France and established the Novelty Glass Co. Victor had been born in Lorraine, France and had learned the glass blowers trade in that country. One of the chief products in the early days of the company were lamp chimneys. This product had an edge in Ottawa because of another immigrant from France named Chappelle. Although the lamp chimneys were blown and looked fragile, Chappelle had arrived with a secret process of tempering the glass so that it could withstand a considerable amount of abuse. Shortly thereafter the Peltier factory began producing an opalescent art glass. This glass was made into library lamp shades, Pullman car windows, and other decorative pieces. Also produced at this time were such grandiose items as cathedral windows.

Eventually Victor was succeeded in the business by his sons Sellers and Joseph. It was under Sellers's leadership that the company first started to produce marbles in the late 1920s. The machines used by Peltier were patented by William J. Miller in 1926 for a design submitted in 1924 (Randall and Webb, 1988). These same machines were apparently used by the Nivison-Weiskopf Co. of Cincinnati from 1921 to 1924. Nivison-Weiskopf is one of the companies producing marbles in the 1920s about which we have virtually no information. The little information we do have comes from the court records of a patent suit brought by the Akro Agate Co. against Master Marble in 1933 (Randall and Webb, 1988). These records state that the machine was built in 1919 to 1920 and delivered to the Nivison-Weiskopf Co. in 1920 by W.J. Miller. In 1923 Nivison-Weiskopf produced over 1,300,000 marbles, although the type of marbles is unknown. Apparently this company stopped producing marbles in January of 1924. It is interesting that the patent for this machine was not applied for until December of 1924, after production at the Nivison-Weiskopf factory had ceased.

At about this point in time Peltier must have purchased either the machines or the right to use the patent design. Randall and Webb (1988) state that in the fiscal year 1928 Peltier produced 33,000,000 marbles. A letter I received in 1965 from Mrs. Meta E. Gundersen told of an interview she had with Mr. Sellers Peltier in 1933, when she was a high school junior doing an English essay on "Early Industries in My County." Mrs. Gundersen provided the text from that essay, which among other things, stated: "For the last six years this factory has been engaged in the making of marbles." That would place the start of marble production at Peltier in 1927. Akro Agate commenced a patent suit against Peltier and their machine in 1929. While production of marbles might have started at Peltier in late 1924 or early 1925 after production had ceased at Nivison-Weiskopf, it is unlikely that Akro Agate would have waited so long to take action. Thus a starting date of 1927 seems more likely.

In any event the patent suit, in which Akro charged that the Miller machine infringed on Hill's patent, was watched with great interest by the marble making community. Originally the suit was decided in favor of Akro, but Peltier appealed to the U.S. circuit court. The appeals court then reversed the earlier decision with an interesting argument. Basically they said that Hill should never have received the patent, because his rollers were not a significant advance over the earlier Christensen machine. They pointed out that Hill was not the first to use helically grooved rollers nor was he the first to use them for making spheres. Since the Hill patent was invalid and the Christensen patent had expired, Peltier had free reign to use machines similar to that used by Akro. Of course, not only did Peltier have the right to use such machines, but so did anyone else. This action coming in 1929 opened the door for a new group of marble companies to start production in the 1930s.

While Peltier made a variety of marbles, the most famous and the most unique are undoubtedly the comic strip marbles. These marbles, called picture marbles by the Peltier Glass Co., were described in company advertising as follows: "Includes the famous movie screen and daily paper comic characters that every child reads and knows about . . . Orphan Annie, Skeezix, Sandy, Betty Boop, Koko, Bimbo, Moon Mullins, Herbie, Andy Gump, Kayo, Emma and Smitty! Each box contains marbles in different color combinations . . . and each marble with a DIFFERENT CHARACTER!" The same advertisement urged dealers to offer them while they were "hot." The ad illustrated a box of twelve marbles similar to that at the center of Plate 31, and suggested the box retail for 25 cents. The same ad also mentioned a box with five marbles which was to retail for 10 cents. The advertisement that I have been referring to begins with the words "Just Out!" in giant print followed in slightly smaller type by the words "marbles with printed comic characters!" Randall and Webb (1988) refer to this same advertisement and date it as 1928. The copy that I have has no date on the advertisement itself, but typed on the side are the words "copy of original artwork, 1938." Either these marbles were "just out" for a long time or one of the two dates is in error. Of course I wouldn't put it past a marble company, particularly in that time period, to use that type of hyperbole for a ten year period. However, it is more likely that one or both of these dates is incorrect.

Randall and Webb (1988) also provide information on how Peltier secured the rights to the process of applying a decal to the surface of marbles. Obviously such a process was novel for the time because Peltier's advertisement states: "Comic characters realistically and permanently decorated on the marbles . . . WILL NOT COME OFF!" This technique was developed by George W. Angerstein of Chicago, who sold the rights to use his procedure to Peltier. Mr. Angerstein signed the contractual agreement with Peltier and applied for a patent on the process in October of 1933. While production of these marbles may have started prior to the signed agreement, it seems unlikely that there would have been a time lag of more than a year. It also seems unlikely that release of these marbles to the market would have been delayed until 1938.

Jim Davis, a Louisiana collector, first came up with the idea of researching the comic strip characters themselves to try to calculate a date for the production of comic strip marbles. The best character for dating purposes turns out to be Betty Boop, one of the stable of Max Fleischer characters, which also included Bimbo and Koko. Max and his brother Dave were famous animators whose cartoons include the still very popular Popeye the Sailor. While Koko's starring role lasted only from 1923 through 1929, Bimbo went on from the 1920s into the 1930s. Betty Boop, or rather the forerunner of her character, started in the late 1920s. However that nameless character looked more like a dog than a female. Sources differ about the first appearance of Betty with the cute vamp-like face appearing on the marble; this happened either in a 1931 cartoon called "Betty Coed," or in a 1932 cartoon called "Stopping the Show." In the latter cartoon she was apparently assisted by Koko and Bimbo, who were now relegated to supporting roles. Betty's period of real popularity began in 1932 and lasted through 1938. The Betty

Boop cartoon "Riding the Rails" received an Oscar nomination in 1938. The picture of Betty Boop used on the marble could not have been produced prior to 1931 and probably not until 1932. Thus the 1933 agreement date between Peltier and Angerstein looks to be about right for the selection of Betty Boop as one of the characters featured on the marble. Therefore it now appears that Peltier's comic strip marbles were probably first released for sale somewhere between 1932 and 1934.

In my previous price guide, I priced Betty, Kayo, and Moon higher than the other characters. This would indicate that these are harder to find or rarer than the others. Since many of these marbles were originally packaged as sets of twelve, original production amounts of the different types might be expected to be about the same. However, despite the original ad claim that all the characters would be different, many original boxes contained two of one of the common characters, thereby leaving out one of the rare ones. One box of twelve had two Andys, two Bimbos, and two Moons, and another had three Andys. Bimbo, Emma, Herbie, and Smitty are the most common figures, with the rest of the comics bringing a premium of some type. Kayo is currently valued the highest.

Also note from the advertisement that these marbles appeared in several different color combinations including such colors as red, blue, green, and black on both a white and yellow base. Some color combinations may thus be rarer than others, however that research has not been done to my knowledge. Very few marbles were made with the figures outlined in red rather than black; these are extremely scarce. Two other decal marbles were also produced by Peltier. One featured Tom Mix, the famous cowboy star, and another was apparently an advertising marble for Cote's Bakery (Plate 30, upper center). The latter marble featured a picture of a baker and had the words Cote's Master Loaf on it. These two marbles were not produced as part of the original sets and are extremely rare compared with the others. Besides the comic strip marbles probably the most famous 1920s marble produced by Peltier were the "Cerise Agates" (Plate 31, center left), an imitation onyx more orange in color than the "Cardinal Reds" of Akro Agate.

8

Marble Games and Toys

Traditional Games

The marble game played for championships and most commonly for entertainment was that of Ring Taw. Taws were the prized stone shooters of the 1800s. The word alabaster, which was used to make marbles, may have been shortened to alley-tor and then to alleys or taws, or the name taw could have come from the word "tor" which is Celtic for rock or stone. Ring Taw is the game used for the annual marble championship of England, which is one of the oldest sporting events in the kingdom. The event was held each year at Tinsley Green. It has existed through eighteen reigns since the year 1588. Traditionally the games are held in the courtyard of the Greyhound Inn on Good Friday. Eight teams participate with six men on a team. The first prize for this event was a suckling pig, the second prize a barrel of beer. In fact, Good Friday in England was once celebrated as Marbles Day. One theory is that this was a ploy by the English clergy who considered a country-wide marbles day preferable to more boisterous and undesirable behavior.

In order to play Ring Taw a circle is drawn on the playing surface. Each player puts a marble in the ring, making sure that they are equally distant from each other. A straight line is marked off some 6' or 7' from the ring. The players would have to shoot from this line which is called the offing, bar, or balk. Then one player "knuckles down" or sets his shooting hand firmly on the line and shoots his taw or shooter at the marbles in the ring. If one of the marbles is knocked out of the ring it belongs to the player who knocked it out, and he may shoot again from the spot where his taw came to rest. As soon as the first player fails to knock a marble out of the ring it is the next player's turn.

There is one more important aspect of the game. If the taw of any player remains in the ring after the shot, that player is out of the game. He must also replace all of the marbles he has won plus one extra by way of a fine. Also, if a later player can hit the taw of one of his opponents, that opponent must give all the marbles he has won to that point to this player. Since having the first shot is a great advantage, the players usually lag for it. Whoever can shoot his taw closest to the center of the circle from the offing line wins the first shot.

This same marble game is still played today. Instead of Ring Taw the game is now called Ringer but the rules are basically the same. The first player to shoot seven marbles out of the ring wins. When the seventh marble is shot out, the shooter marble must also leave the ring. If this does not happen, the seventh marble is placed back in the ring.

Bridge Board is an example of an old target game. Nine arches were cut in a piece of wood, each arch being labeled with a number from 0 to 9. The lowest numbers were always toward the middle with the highest numbers toward either end. When the board was placed on the ground the arches allowed paths through the board large enough for a marble. The players shot at the bridge board from a given distance. For each shot the player would pay one person designated as the banker one marble. If the taw passed through one of the arches the player would receive from the banker the number of marbles equal to the number written over the arch. When the taw did not pass through an arch the player would receive nothing. And if the taw missed the bridge board altogether the player paid another marble as a fine.

Three Holes, another target game, was at one time very popular in England. Three small holes were formed in a row, each hole being about 2″ in diameter and 1″ in depth. The distance between the holes could be 3′ or 4′ or even more depending upon the skill of the players. A line was drawn about a yard from the first hole. As soon as a player succeeded with the first hole he could try for the next hole. Whenever a player won a hole he received a marble from each of the other players. The first player to put his taw in all three holes won the game. If one player hit the taw of another player, the player whose taw had been hit was out of the game and had to forfeit all of the marbles he had won to the player who hit his marble.

A miniature version of Bowls used marbles and was called Spanners. One player would shoot his marble out a distance of a few yards as a target for his opponent. It is interesting to note that the marbles are to be shot with the thumb rather than rolled or thrown. If the other player can hit the first player's marble, he wins one marble. He can also win a marble by placing his taw close enough to his opponent's that the distance between them can be spanned by the fingers and thumb of one hand. Attempting to win by the span is quite dangerous, for if you fail, your opponent is in an excellent position to either hit or obtain a span with your marble.

Another game which has been played with marbles since the early English period is that of Conqueror. One player lays his taw on the ground and the other throws his own taw at it with all his force. If the target taw breaks, the other taw is known as the conqueror. One half of the broken taw is then taken as a trophy by the conqueror. If the target taw does not break it is then thrown at the other taw. When one taw breaks another that has previously broken other marbles, all the marbles which have been broken earlier are also added to the winning taw's score. For instance, if my taw had broken twenty marbles and it breaks your taw which had also broken twenty marbles, then my taw will rank as a conqueror of 41. Now you know what happened to all of those valuable early marbles and why antique marbles in good condition are so hard to find today.

Board Games

GAMES OF STRATEGY

The forerunners of marble-using board games may have an origin older than that of marbles themselves. One game consisting of a double row of six shallow depressions in a board or stone has been found in excavations dating to thousands of years before the birth of Christ. This game was purportedly played by Cleopatra and is still played throughout Africa and India today. Play begins with four nuts, stones, or marbles in each depression. The beginning player selects a starting point, scoops the marbles up from a depression, and then drops them one by one into the depressions in a clockwise movement. He continues to play in this fashion until he reaches an emptied depression, at which point his opponent's turn begins. A player scores points when he puts the fourth marble into a previously emptied depression. Thus this is a tactical game in which players of equal skill can often counter each other's moves.

In Ghana this game is called Oware, which literally means "he marries." Ghanian folklore tells of a man and woman who began a game of Oware. They were evenly matched and neither could get an advantage. Thus they eventually decided to marry, since that was the only way they could spend enough time together to finish the game. My game board, which comes from Ghana, is carved from two semi-circular pieces of wood which are hinged together at the base. Therefore, the circular board can be folded in half, latched shut, and carried like a briefcase by its carved handles. On one of the outside faces of the wood are carved the heads of a man and woman, a reference to how the game received its name.

The solitaire or General Grant games are perhaps the best known board games from the 1800s which use marbles. Certainly these games were manufactured into the 1900s, and they can be reproduced today, again making the acquisition of some history along with the marble board a good idea when purchasing one. Such a game was pictured on the cover of the marbles pamphlet published by Morrison and Terison. On the back of their booklet they refer to it as "General Grant's Marble Game," and state that it was carried and played by Union soldiers during the Civil War. This information may be correct. Certainly there is evidence that this game was in use during the period of the Civil War in the 1860s. In fact, the game standing upright in the lower right of Plate 32 has an inscription written in script on the underside of the board apparently giving the name of the owner and adding, "London, 1864." Another such game is traceable to David Dresbach, the first director or mayor of the town of Circleville, Ohio. Mr. Dresbach held this position for almost forty years between 1810 and 1850. That such games were still popular at the turn of the century is evidenced by the 1902 Sears Roebuck and Co. catalog where "solitaire boards" were advertised as: "Made of polished hardwood, and varnished; 38 glass marbles with each board . . . A very interesting and always an acceptable game." The board and marbles together cost 48 cents.

Both the 1902 Sears Roebuck and Co. board and the board at lower left in Plate 32 have wooden trays which swivel out from underneath the primary game board in which the marbles can be kept. Some smaller and plainer but verifiably older games do not have such a swing out marble holder. Also note that most of these game boards have a groove around the outside edge in which marbles can be placed as they are removed from the board and which also catches marbles that might roll accidentally from the board. Another interesting feature of many of the early boards is the series of lines, double lines, and the colored border surrounding the nine holes at one end of the cross pattern, such as the green border and lines present in the game board pictured in the lower center of Plate 32. This pattern is also on the other game boards in Plate 32, although the color is much fainter. The border and lines were used to play the game German Tactics.

At least three different games were played on the old solitaire game boards. The most common of these, of course, was solitaire itself. Games with the same pattern of depressions using either pegs or marbles are still manufactured today. The game starts with marbles or pegs in all of the holes except the center hole. The object of the game is to eliminate marbles or pegs by jumping vertically or horizontally and to end with only a single marble or peg in the center hole. Accomplishing this feat is not easy! Often these games have been sold in recent years as "I.Q. games" where one could progress from a dimwit to a genius by leaving fewer and fewer pegs or marbles. Two other games were listed in a booklet entitled "Rules for the Compendium of Games," which from its cover and contents appears to date from the 1860s to the mid 1880s. This book lists rules for backgammon, chess, cribbage, dominos, draughts, solitaire, and whist among others. The others include two games played on the solitaire board, Fox and Geese and German Tactics. Both of these latter games were played by two individuals. In Fox and Geese one person had a single marble, the fox, which was in the center hole. Seventeen other marbles representing geese occupied one half of the board with the exception of the holes on either side of the fox. Foxes and geese can move along any of the lines with the fox moving first. The fox can eliminate a goose if it can jump over the marble and land in a vacant hole behind it. If the fox can reduce the number of geese to six he has won the game. If, however, the geese are successful in blocking the fox so he cannot move, they win the game.

The popularity of the game German Tactics is evident from the fact that most of the early solitaire boards have the required pattern needed for the game painted on the board. One of the two players has two marbles which are officers and the other has 24 marbles representing ordinary soldiers. The two officers may be placed on any two of the holes within the garrison, the garrison being that portion of the board within the colored square. The 24 men fill the 24 holes that are outside of the color pattern. It is the ordinary soldiers who are the first to advance. Officers are permitted to advance or retreat along both the single and double lines. Once again the officers may take one of the men by jumping over him into a vacant hole and in fact in this game may take several men at one move. On the other hand the men cannot take the officers; they can only advance, and they can only advance along the single lines. The rules state that the officers win the game by reducing the men to eight in number, by having the men so disposed that they are unable to move, or by one or both officers themselves being blockaded in the garrison so they are unable to move. This is a twist, since this result in the Fox and Geese game gives the game to the geese. In German Tactics, however, the only way for the men to win the game is by taking possession of all of the holes within the garrison. Of course this means that it would be difficult for both officers to leave the garrison, since they might be blocked from returning.

Solitaire boards, as shown in Plate 32, come in a variety of sizes. Marbles associated with these boards likewise came in a variety of sizes. It is always risky business to assume that the marbles being sold with a particular board were original to that board. In my opinion the boards themselves have an intrinsic value (being fairly rare), whether or not any marbles are present with the board. Only in a few unusual cases have I been reasonably certain that the marbles coming with an individual game board were original. One such board is a small one which was purchased from an Amish family in Pennsylvania by Lloyd Huffer and then sold to me. With this board were 32 small blue micas, all exactly the same size and all with similar pontil marks. The fact that these marbles were smaller than the normal playing size, were perfectly matched by color and pontil mark, and were purchased directly from the family in which the board had been an heirloom, all lead me to believe that they were the original marbles with the board. It is unlikely that anyone could round up 32 blue micas of that size, even if they had the inclination to do so. Once again, however, the best way to add value to your collection is to obtain as much history as you can with each purchase, and then write down the details before you forget them.

GAMES OF CHANCE

Pinball and its ancestor bagatelle also have a large army of collectors and a considerable history. In fact I recently purchased the book *Pinball One* by Richard M. Bueschel (1988) which is 246 pages and billed as the first volume of 10. Thank goodness I'm not writing about pinball machines! Bueschel relates that the origins of bagatelle go back over 300 years to the time of Shakespeare and the waning of the Elizabethan period in England.

By the mid to late 1500s a miniaturized version of the game nine pins was being played on tables in inns. Sometime shortly before 1600 an unknown entrepreneur had a great idea. Instead of nine pins he put nine shallow holes or pockets in the location where the pins had been. Not only did this speed up the action, since no longer did the pins have to be reset, but it required more skill since the hand rolled balls had to have the correct speed not to overshoot the pocket. This basic game then evolved in two different directions. One of these was into billiards and pool, the word billiard coming from the French word *billiart*, or "little stick." Billiards had actually been co-evolving in France during the 1500s from what started as a table top version of croquet. The second direction for the evolution of nine holes was to the game of bagatelle and from there to games of pinball.

Bueschel (1988) conjectures that the first true bagatelle game may have been invented by the Count Conte d'Artois, the youngest brother of the ill-fated King Louis XVI. According to Langed (1903) the young Count "was the most extravagant prince of his time. He had a number of domains, was a gambler, a betting man and constantly in money difficulties, and his brother, Louis XVI, had several times to pay his heavy debts." A year after Louis XVI ascended to the throne his young brother petitioned him for the estate of Chateau d'Bagatelle, a run-down property on the outskirts of Paris. The Count d'Artois bet the queen, Marie Antoinette, that he would be able to build a new mansion within seven weeks, in time for a party when the king returned to Versailles from western France. Employing 900 workers day and night the Count managed to win this seemingly impossible bet.

The lawn party, given in the summer of 1777 when the Count was 20 years old, was one of the major social events of Louis XVI's reign. The new Chateau d'Bagatelle included, among numerous other luxuries, a "salon de jeu" or game room. The new betting game of bagatelle appeared on the French scene at almost this exact time. Thus it is easy to conjecture that either the Count himself invented the game or that at least he financially supported its development and had it displayed in his new game room. Bagatelle chiefly differed from its ancestor nine holes by having an inclined playing field, and by having the pockets shielded by nails or pins. Thus one now had to shoot the balls into the pockets indirectly, arching them up towards the top and then having them come back down into the pockets. All that separates this game from pinball is the addition of a glass cover and a spring action plunger to hit the balls.

By the mid 1800s the large scale bagatelle games, which were meant as adult gambling entertainments, started to give rise to smaller tabletop versions used as children's toys. Bueschel (1988) mentions that many of these early games used the clay marbles, which would have been inexpensive for the game makers to purchase. The Montgomery Ward and Co. catalog in 1899 lists three sizes of "improved bagatelle boards." The cheapest, at 25 cents, had one bell, a star, two pockets, three marbles, and eight places for the marbles to count. The largest, 75 cents, had seven metal pockets, one large and two small nickeled bells, and a star which revolved when hit. A related game listed on the same page was Spinette or Flip, listed as "an amusing game or occupation for the little ones; they enjoy chasing the marbles into their places by spinning the totem or button top with their fingers."

Montague Redgrave had immigrated from England to America, arriving in Cincinnati in 1869 (Bueschel, 1988). A year later he had applied for a patent which would make him known as the father of pinball. Redgrave was the one who added the spring-loaded shooter to the game of bagatelle. The 1902 Sears Roebuck catalog featured a number of Redgrave bagatelle boards for children. The descriptions in the 1902 Sears catalog are so close to those in the 1899 Montgomery Ward catalog that it is almost certain the Montgomery Ward bagatelle boards were also manufactured by Redgrave. However, by 1902 Redgrave apparently had become enough of a "brand name" to make the mention of the manufacturer worthwhile in the advertisement in the catalog. The only other difference in the ads is that now the larger game cost $1 and that the marbles were specified as being made of glass. Glass marbles in this era would either have to have been imported or would have had to come from Navarre in 1899 or from Christensen in 1902. Of course many later versions of these pinball games occurred during the 1930s, 1940s, and 1950s and are now becoming collectible. As with all collectibles, condition is of primary importance in the value of these items.

Other Games and Toys

Of course marble games were not limited to games of solitaire or bagatelle. Marbles were an integral part of a wide variety of creative games. The Marble Muggins game pictured on the upper left of Plate 32 is a straight adaptation of outdoor shooting games in which the marbles were shot at arches or holes in the ground. The colorful Muggins cardboard with its arches was attached to the bottom of the box on one end, allowing it to be pulled out slightly and stood up. The game was manufactured by the American Toy Manufacturing Co. in Salem, Massachusetts. Instructions on the box suggest that players shoot from 6' away and that each player have ten marbles. Although no date is given on this toy, it probably was manufactured around the turn of the century. Another straight forward toy pictured in the center of Plate 32 consisted of a series of inclined wooden troughs down which marbles could be rolled. Modern versions of this game, often employing more sophisticated twists and turns in plastic, are still being manufactured and sold today. These games hold a real fascination for young children, although they appear to be very simple to an adult. (My son Brendan, who was about $3\frac{1}{2}$ years old when I wrote this, spent a great deal of time rolling marbles down this old toy. This is particularly surprising since Brendan was much more an active chase and play type than a game type.) The toy pictured was manufactured by the Oster Manufacturing Co., and again a date of around the turn of the century is probably likely, although the toy itself is not dated.

Another simple toy was the one called Gloria Mosaic. It was manufactured in Germany and has the name Brillant near the trademark on the cover. This was the game which used the metallic colored clay marbles featured in Plate 2. The game, if it could be called that, was simply a series of cardboard squares with different patterns of holes punched in them. Along with the game came a booklet of colored pictures showing possible colorful patterns that could be produced by putting different colored marbles into the different holes. Thus this was not an active play game but rather a "construct a picture" game. The age of this game is probably much later than those others I have been discussing. Even though data is again lacking, I suspect that this game may have been produced in the 1930s.

Another single player game was entitled The Three Blind Mice and had a trademark registered in 1889. The game consisted of a small round box within which was a series of cardboard concentric circles having offset openings, in other words a sort of maze. In the center was a "trap," another cardboard circle with a cover of wood and a single opening. The box contained some verses of The Three Blind Mice song and then the following instructions: "Put three mice (marbles) into the outer circle. The game is to handle the board as to get all of the mice into the trap together, without touching them. After three mice can be readily caught, interest will be added to the game by putting in four or five." Three Blind Mice, then, was a forerunner of all those games, many still being sold today, in which small balls have to be maneuvered into holes by tilting and turning a hand held (and now often plastic covered) board. This original game came with several small brown Bennington marbles.

The Panama Pile Drivers featured in Plate 32 (top) were more of an action toy. The original version was patented in 1905 and the more elaborate version with the man in the cart was patented in 1914. In the first version the marbles (clay) being carried up and down caused a metal weight or pile driver to rise and fall. In the second version a man in a cart went up and down as a counter balance to the marbles (now hollow steel balls with a cross-mark on them). One wonders why this second version was still called the Panama Pile Driver, since the pile driver had been replaced by a cart. At the extreme end of the action toy spectrum was a brass cannon measuring over a foot long. This cannon is inscribed with the words "young America rapid fire gun" and was patented in February of 1907. It had large spoked wheels on either side with which it could be rolled across the floor. The cannon barrel itself was sort of a double barrel or an over-under affair; marbles are loaded into the top and then dropped one at a time into the lower barrel, where by turning a crank the marbles were fired at surprising speed and force out of the cannon. I can well imagine that this toy had a very short lived existence in many households. Its obviously superior capability to destroy fragile heirlooms and to inflict serious torture on younger brothers and sisters should have been enough to have most parents trash it within several days of arrival. Thus while I am no great judge of rarity in toys, I would be very surprised if many of these "young America rapid fire guns" survived.

Undoubtedly there are hundreds of other toys and games which used marbles over the last 150 years. I do not pretend that this chapter is either all encompassing or even succeeds in listing the major varieties. Nor will I make any attempt to price toys or games in this book. Such items have a double circle of collectors. They are not only sought by marble collectors but also by toy collectors, who are probably even more numerous than marble collectors. Marble collectors who want to start collecting these sorts of items should start going to some of the toy shows and familiarize themselves with prices in the toy market. Disclaimers aside, such marble novelty items are fun to own, and I hope this chapter stimulates some interest in their collection.

Other Uses: Education and the Ballot Box

There is always the eccentric who is ahead of his time in promoting marbles as an educational toy rather than just a form of entertainment. In *Appletons' Journal* of 1869 mention is made of "that famous old man" Dr. Cornelius Scriblerus. This gentleman wanted his son Martinus to have only the very best toys, meaning those "such as might prove of use to his mind, by instilling an early notion of the sciences." Luckily, marbles were among the selected few, since Dr. Scriblerus believed they taught his son percussion and the laws of motion. Some of the other toys which the good doctor managed to take the fun out of included nutcrackers, which taught the use of the lever; bird cages, which taught the use of the pulley; and tops, which taught centrifugal motion. Luckily most children are very resilient and will survive this type of treatment with no major damage being done.

I really have no information on the origins of the ballot box, although it certainly has been in use for a long time. Ballot boxes were small wooden affairs with a short straight handle on one end, allowing them to be carried with one hand (Plate 32, upper right). On the end of the box opposite the handle was an open tray which could be filled with white and black marbles. The other end of the box had a covered compartment with a single small opening into which a marble could be dropped. The lid on this half could be lifted later to retrieve the marbles. A large number of societies used these boxes to vote on new members or other matters. The box would be presented to a member who would reach in and conceal a black or white marble in his hand. He would then slip the marble into the covered compartment of the box. Thus no one would know his vote, and no one except the officers who opened the sealed compartment would know the total vote. The term "black ball" derives from the fact that the black marbles indicated a No vote or a vote against admitting someone to membership. In many secret societies, private clubs, or fraternities and sororities, a single No vote or "black ball" would be sufficient to bar a potential new member from joining the group.

Over the period of years that they existed, ballot boxes used both white and black opaque glass marbles cut from canes (Plate 18B, right circle, center), and white and black glazed crockery marbles related to the Bennington variety (Plate 2, center). Usually in membership votes more white balls were required than black balls. Thus it is not surprising that black opaque marbles are rarer than white opaque marbles. However what is somewhat surprising is that the black balls were originally more expensive. In a sporting goods catalog produced by E.I. Horsman of New York in the spring of 1893 a secret ballot box made from black walnut is advertised at $3 if finished in oil and $4 if finished with a "fine French polish." Also advertised are extra white ballot balls at 40 cents per hundred and extra black ballot balls at 60 cents per hundred. Apparently the black opaque glass was more expensive than the white. Once again the ballot box is an item that has probably been produced up to the present time, thus necessitating the same advice given for numerous previous items of obtaining some history with your purchase if possible.

Price Guide

Please read the section in the Introduction on pricing marbles—it covers topics such as rarity and condition. Remember at all times that this is a price *guide* not a price list. The purpose of the guide is to give you a feeling for the relative worth of different types of marbles in today's market. Please feel free to buy lower and sell higher, if you can. (I'll certainly try to!) Prices may vary in different regions, but the relative value of the different types should remain about the same. Through time even these may change; as a general rule rarer, more valuable marbles tend to appreciate faster than common, less valuable ones.

I was greatly assisted in compiling this price guide by Don Taylor of Ann Arbor, Michigan. Don routinely buys and sells (i.e. deals in) marbles. Without his awareness of current market conditions, this guide would not have been possible. Bob Hutchison supplied pricing information for Peltier comic strip marbles, and Brian Estepp provided valuable advice on pricing other types of machine-made marbles. However, as much as I might wish otherwise, the final prices appearing here are my responsibility (for better or worse). Marble prices are those paid for marbles in mint condition (or darn close to it). In other words, there should be no damage to the marble. Remember that prices will also vary based on the individual marble's intrinsic beauty. Sizes given are the diameter of the marble.

Some types of marbles currently sell for less than their rarity and beauty would seem to indicate. Often these are unusual subgroups of marbles that have not been recognized as a separate "type" by most of the collecting public, and/or which have not previously been priced separately in a guide. I am taking the liberty (risk?) of marking with an asterisk some groups of marbles that I believe to be undervalued compared to most of the marbles being priced. Admittedly this is only one person's opinion, and, like a stockbroker's advice, it is your money that is on the line, not mine—I make no guarantees about the appreciation of marbles in these groups. Also notice that not all the subgroups or color patterns separated in the text tables are listed separately in the price guide. The reasons for this are too varied to discuss here. Suffice it to say that those collectors who use the text and tables along with the price guide should have an advantage over those using the price guide alone.

A word about pricing sulphides. Please read the text section on sulphide marbles before using the price guide! Sulphides are priced as average size ($1\frac{5}{8}''$) in mint (or "real near mint") condition with a good clear figure. As stated in the text, I don't pay much of a premium for size in sulphides, but others might. In a sample of 88 sulphides, $1\frac{5}{8}''$ was the median size. Marbles either much larger or much smaller than that were produced in lesser amounts. My list of figures is not meant to be exhaustive, only representative. Very rare sulphides, like other very rare marbles, can only be given sort of a base or "ball park" price. Actual prices paid will depend on who the principal bidders are and how they feel on that given day. The prices of those unusual sulphide figures listing at $1,000 or more in this guide are actually based on auction prices (or often a single auction price) paid for that figure within the last few years. Thus these values are less reliable than those for more common figures. As explained in the text, I believe there are bargains available in the sulphide marble market for those who are educated buyers.

Best of luck in your collecting!

PRICES BY MARBLE SIZE IN DOLLARS

Location	Color	$\frac{1}{2}''$	$\frac{5}{8}''$	$\frac{3}{4}''$	$\frac{7}{8}''$	$1''$	$1\frac{1}{4}''$	$1\frac{1}{2}''$	$1\frac{3}{4}''$	$2''$	$2\frac{1}{4}+''$	$2\frac{1}{2}''$

STONE

Limestone

Location	Color	$\frac{1}{2}''$	$\frac{5}{8}''$	$\frac{3}{4}''$	$\frac{7}{8}''$	$1''$	$1\frac{1}{4}''$	$1\frac{1}{2}''$	$1\frac{3}{4}''$	$2''$	$2\frac{1}{4}+''$	$2\frac{1}{2}''$
Plate 1, center right	Natural	1.00	1.00	2.00	5.00	10.00						
Plate 1, top and top right	Colored	3.00	3.00	5.00	7.50	15.00						

Agate

Location	Color	$\frac{1}{2}''$	$\frac{5}{8}''$	$\frac{3}{4}''$	$\frac{7}{8}''$	$1''$	$1\frac{1}{4}''$	$1\frac{1}{2}''$	$1\frac{3}{4}''$	$2''$	$2\frac{1}{4}+''$	$2\frac{1}{2}''$
Plate 1	Natural (unbanded)	5.00	5.00	6.00	7.00	10.00						
Plate 1, left center and center	Natural (banded)	12.00	12.00	16.00	25.00	35.00	60.00	85.00				
Plate 1, upper left and center	Colored	40.00	40.00	65.00	90.00	115.00	150.00	200.00				

Semiprecious Stone

Location	Color	$\frac{1}{2}''$	$\frac{5}{8}''$	$\frac{3}{4}''$	$\frac{7}{8}''$	$1''$	$1\frac{1}{4}''$	$1\frac{1}{2}''$	$1\frac{3}{4}''$	$2''$	$2\frac{1}{4}+''$	$2\frac{1}{2}''$
Plate 1, lower left	Tigereye	30.00	30.00	35.00	40.00	55.00						
Plate 1, lower right	Bloodstone and Rose Quartz	45.00	45.00	50.00	60.00	80.00	125.00					

CLAY, CROCKERY, AND CHINA

Clay

Location	Color	$\frac{1}{2}''$	$\frac{5}{8}''$	$\frac{3}{4}''$	$\frac{7}{8}''$	$1''$	$1\frac{1}{4}''$	$1\frac{1}{2}''$	$1\frac{3}{4}''$	$2''$	$2\frac{1}{4}+''$	$2\frac{1}{2}''$
Plate 2, upper left	Natural	0.30	0.30	0.50	1.25	2.00	4.00	8.00				
Plate 2, upper left	Colored	0.40	0.40	0.75	2.00	4.00	8.00	15.00				
* Plate 2, top right and upper center	Rolled and Birds Egg	0.60	0.60	1.00	2.50	5.00	10.00	20.00				

151

PRICES BY MARBLE SIZE IN DOLLARS

Location	Color	1/2"	5/8"	3/4"	7/8"	1"	1¼"	1½"	1¾"	2"	2¼+"	2½"
Pipe Clay												
Plate 2, left center	Lined	0.50	0.50	1.00	2.00	7.00	15.00	25.00				
Plate 2, left center	Leaf/Bullseye	0.75	0.75	1.50	4.00	10.00	18.00	30.00				
Crockery												
Plate 2, lower left	Brown Bennington	0.50	0.50	1.00	2.00	4.00	8.00	15.00	30.00	60.00		
Plate 2, center right	Blue Bennington	0.75	0.75	1.50	3.00	5.00	12.00	25.00	50.00	80.00		
Plate 2, lower right	Fancy Bennington	2.00	2.00	4.00	6.00	12.00	25.00	50.00	80.00	120.00		
Plate 2, center	White Ballot	1.00	1.00	1.00								
Plate 2, center	Black Ballot	2.00	2.00	2.00								
* Plate 3, lower center	Fancy Pinks	8.00	8.00	15.00	30.00	50.00						
* Plate 3, upper right and center	American Majolica	5.00	5.00	9.00	12.00	25.00						
Plate 3, lower left	Lined Crockery (blue & green on white)	6.00	6.00	10.00	15.00	28.00	40.00	70.00				
Plate 3, upper left	Lined Crockery (single color on white)	10.00	10.00	15.00	25.00	40.00	60.00	90.00				
Plate 3, upper left	Lined Crockery (pink or colored base)	15.00	15.00	25.00	35.00	50.00	75.00					
Plate 3, upper center	Patched or Coil	30.00	30.00	45.00	60.00	90.00	125.00					
Plate 3, right center	Spattered Crockery	3.50	3.50	5.00	8.00	12.00	25.00					
Plate 3, bottom right	Stoneware	5.00	5.00	12.00	20.00	40.00	75.00	120.00	180.00	250.00		
China												
Plate 4, top center and left	Intersecting Helixes	7.00	6.00	10.00	15.00	28.00	40.00	85.00				
Plate 4, upper right	Bullseyes (thin)	8.00	8.00	12.00	18.00	30.00	50.00	100.00				
Plate 4, upper left	Leaf with Coil or Helix	8.00	8.00	15.00	20.00	40.00	65.00	120.00				
Plate 4, lower right	Intersecting Lines Solid and	10.00	10.00	18.00	25.00	45.00	75.00	135.00				
Plate 4, center column	Doughnut Bullseyes	25.00	20.00	30.00	45.00	70.00	100.00	150.00				

PRICES BY MARBLE SIZE IN DOLLARS

Location	Color	$\frac{1}{2}$"	$\frac{5}{8}$"	$\frac{3}{4}$"	$\frac{7}{8}$"	1"	$1\frac{1}{4}$"	$1\frac{1}{2}$"	$1\frac{3}{4}$"	2"	$2\frac{1}{4}$ +"	$2\frac{1}{2}$"
Plate 5, upper	Geometrics	25.00	25.00	35.00	60.00	100.00	165.00	225.00				
Plate 5, bottom, lower left	Flowers (later)	200.00	200.00	275.00	325.00	400.00	500.00	600.00				
Plate 5, lower right	Flowers (Bullseye, King's Rose, & Pinkies)	250.00	250.00	325.00	400.00	450.00	550.00	650.00				
Plate 5, center	Scenes			3,000 +								

CANE CUT GLASS

Latticinio

Location	Color	$\frac{1}{2}$"	$\frac{5}{8}$"	$\frac{3}{4}$"	$\frac{7}{8}$"	1"	$1\frac{1}{4}$"	$1\frac{1}{2}$"	$1\frac{3}{4}$"	2"	$2\frac{1}{4}$ +"	$2\frac{1}{2}$"
Plate 8, upper	White	10.00	7.50	10.00	15.00	25.00	40.00	60.00	80.00	120.00	180.00	250.00
Plate 8, lower	Yellow	12.00	8.00	12.00	17.50	30.00	45.00	70.00	95.00	140.00	200.00	275.00
* Plate 9	Alternating (white & yellow)	25.00	20.00	25.00	35.00	50.00	75.00	110.00	160.00	220.00	280.00	
* Plate 9, center and Plate 28E	Red or orange, alone or with other colors	45.00	40.00	65.00	90.00	130.00	175.00	250.00	400.00	550.00	750.00	
* Plate 9, upper center and right and Plate 28D	Banded, ribbon, or tri-level	85.00	75.00	100.00	125.00	160.00	200.00	250.00	400.00	550.00	750.00	

Solid Core

Location	Color	$\frac{1}{2}$"	$\frac{5}{8}$"	$\frac{3}{4}$"	$\frac{7}{8}$"	1"	$1\frac{1}{4}$"	$1\frac{1}{2}$"	$1\frac{3}{4}$"	2"	$2\frac{1}{4}$ +"	$2\frac{1}{2}$"
Plate 10	White Column	12.50	10.00	12.50	20.00	35.00	48.00	75.00	100.00	150.00	225.00	325.00
* Plate 10, upper right	Yellow Column	15.00	12.50	15.00	25.00	45.00	60.00	95.00	125.00	180.00	260.00	375.00
* Plate 11	Blue, Green, or Red base Column or Tri-level	35.00	30.00	40.00	60.00	100.00	150.00	225.00	325.00	450.00	600.00	
Plate 10, bottom	White Ridged	35.00	30.00	35.00	50.00	75.00	100.00	150.00	185.00	240.00	350.00	500.00
* Plate 10, lower left	Yellow Ridged	45.00	40.00	45.00	60.00	85.00	120.00	175.00	250.00	350.00	475.00	625.00

153

Location	Color	PRICES BY MARBLE SIZE IN DOLLARS										
		$\frac{1}{2}''$	$\frac{5}{8}''$	$\frac{3}{4}''$	$\frac{7}{8}''$	$1''$	$1\frac{1}{4}''$	$1\frac{1}{2}''$	$1\frac{3}{4}''$	$2''$	$2\frac{1}{4}+''$	$2\frac{1}{2}''$
Divided Core												
Plate 12	3 or 4 Strand	12.50	10.00	12.50	20.00	35.00	48.00	75.00	100.00	150.00	225.00	325.00
Ribbon												
Plate 13	Single Ribbon	110.00	80.00	110.00	140.00	175.00	225.00	275.00	330.00	400.00	475.00	
Plate 13	Double Ribbon	70.00	50.00	70.00	100.00	125.00	160.00	200.00	260.00	320.00	380.00	
Lutz												
Plate 15, lower circle	Clear Banded	110.00	90.00	125.00	175.00	250.00	400.00	600.00	850.00	1,200.00	2,500.00	
Plate 15, upper circle	Colored Swirl	135.00	120.00	225.00	350.00	500.00	750.00	1,250.00	1,800.00	3,000.00	4,000.00	
Plate 14, upper right	Ribbon Core	135.00	120.00	250.00	350.00	500.00	750.00	1,250.00	1,800.00	3,000.00	4,000.00	
Plate 15, upper circle	Opaque	225.00	200.00	300.00	450.00	600.00	850.00	1,500.00	2,200.00	3,500.00	4,500.00	
Plate 14	Onionskin	125.00	100.00	225.00	320.00	475.00	700.00	1,250.00	1,800.00	3,000.00	4,000.00	
Colored Glass												
Plate 16	Maypole	45.00	35.00	45.00	80.00	125.00	175.00	300.00				
Plate 17, lower left and center right	Amber Ribbon or Gooseberry	45.00	40.00	50.00	100.00	150.00						
Plate 17, center	Swirl and/or Core	75.00	60.00	90.00	125.00	175.00	250.00	400.00	600.00	850.00	1,200.00	
Plate 16, upper right	Mag-Lites	90.00	85.00	125.00	200.00	325.00	550.00	850.00	1,400.00	3,000.00		
Plate 16, center left	Submarines	120.00	100.00	150.00	225.00	300.00	500.00	850.00				
Plate 16, lower right	Uncolored coreless	45.00	35.00	45.00	80.00	125.00	175.00	300.00				
Mist												
Plate 18, upper half	Mist	85.00	75.00	115.00	180.00	250.00						

154

Location	Color	$\frac{1}{2}''$	$\frac{5}{8}''$	$\frac{3}{4}''$	$\frac{7}{8}''$	1"	$1\frac{1}{4}''$	$1\frac{1}{2}''$	$1\frac{3}{4}''$	2"	$2\frac{1}{4}''+$	$2\frac{1}{2}''$
Ballot and Pastels												
Plate 18, lower right, circle center	Ballot (white)	5.00	5.00	10.00	15.00							
Plate 18, lower right, circle center	Ballot (black)	10.00	10.00	15.00	20.00							
Plate 18, lower half, right circle	Red and Blue Pastel	40.00	40.00	60.00	100.00	180.00	300.00	450.00	750.00	1,250.00	1,800.00	
Plate 18, lower half, right circle	Green, Yellow, Purple, and other Pastel	75.00	75.00	120.00	200.00	250.00	400.00	575.00	900.00	1,500.00	2,200.00	
Clambroths												
Plate 19, center and lower left	Red or Blue Clam (white base)	100.00	85.00	130.00	225.00	350.00	600.00	1,100.00	2,000.00	3,000.00	4,500.00	
Plate 19	White Based Clam (other colors)	120.00	120.00	175.00	300.00	450.00	750.00	1,400.00	2,500.00	3,500.00	5,000.00	
Plate 19, lower right	Black Clam (with white)	120.00	120.00	160.00	275.00	400.00	650.00	1,100.00	1,800.00	2,750.00	4,000.00	
Plate 19, upper center	Pastel Clam	250.00	250.00	325.00	500.00	750.00	1,100.00	1,800.00	3,000.00	4,500.00	6,000.00	
Banded Opaque and Indian												
Plate 20, upper center	Red Banded Opaque	75.00	75.00	115.00	200.00	285.00	425.00	650.00	850.00	1,100.00		
Plate 20, upper right	Banded Opaque (other colors)	85.00	85.00	130.00	225.00	325.00	475.00	750.00	1,000.00	1,250.00		
Plate 20, arc below center	Banded Pastel	200.00	200.00	275.00	425.00	675.00	850.00	1,400.00	2,500.00			
Plate 20	Indians	75.00	75.00	110.00	200.00	325.00	550.00	850.00	1,400.00	3,000.00		
Plate 20, upper far left	Gaudy Black (360° Indian)	275.00	275.00	350.00	500.00	650.00						
Peppermint Swirls												
Plate 18, lower half, left circle	Peppermint	75.00	75.00	90.00	135.00	300.00	500.00	850.00	1,200.00	2,000.00		

PRICES BY MARBLE SIZE IN DOLLARS

Location	Color	$\frac{1}{2}''$	$\frac{5}{8}''$	$\frac{3}{4}''$	$\frac{7}{8}''$	$1''$	$1\frac{1}{4}''$	$1\frac{1}{2}''$	$1\frac{3}{4}''$	$2''$	$2\frac{1}{4}+''$	$2\frac{1}{2}''$
Mica												
Plate 21	Clear, Blue, Green, Amber	20.00	15.00	25.00	45.00	80.00	150.00	300.00	450.00	800.00	1,300.00	
Plate 21, bottom	Red	400.00	400.00	500.00	650.00	900.00						
Onionskin (Mica will increase the value by at least 50%)												
Plate 22	Segmented	35.00	30.00	50.00	75.00	95.00	125.00	165.00	250.00	350.00	475.00	650.00
Plate 23	Single Color	35.00	30.00	50.00	75.00	110.00	150.00	200.00	325.00	450.00	600.00	800.00
Plate 23, lower left	Speckled	45.00	40.00	65.00	90.00	130.00	175.00	250.00	400.00	525.00	700.00	1,000
Plate 23, lower center	Lobed	100.00	100.00	150.00	200.00	250.00	325.00	425.00	550.00	675.00	900.00	1,500.00
Plate 23, center	Joseph Swirl		50.00	75.00	100.00	150.00	200.00	300.00				
INDIVIDUALLY MADE MARBLES												
Plate 25, lower circle	End-of-Day		150.00	190.00	225.00	260.00	350.00	450.00	600.00	725.00	1,000.00	1,800.00
Plate 25, upper center	Cloud		125.00	180.00	250.00	400.00	600.00	900.00				
Plate 25, upper row, left and right	Paperweight							2,500+				
TRANSITION MARBLES												
Plate 29, lower two-thirds	Navarre		25.00	35.00	45.00	75.00	120.00	200.00	275.00	375.00		
Plate 29, upper one-third	Faceted		35.00	50.00	80.00	110.00	150.00					
MACHINE-MADE MARBLES												
Plate 30, upper center	Guinea (clear or cobalt)		150.00	180.00								

PRICES BY MARBLE SIZE IN DOLLARS

Location	Color	$\frac{1}{2}''$	$\frac{5}{8}''$	$\frac{3}{4}''$	$\frac{7}{8}''$	$1''$	$1\frac{1}{4}''$	$1\frac{1}{2}''$	$1\frac{3}{4}''$	$2''$	$2\frac{1}{4}+''$	$2\frac{1}{2}''$
Plate 30, lower center	Flames (red & white)		15.00	30.00								
Plate 30, lower center	Flames (3 or 4 color)		25.00	65.00								
Plate 30, bottom	Slag or Onyx (clear, brown, or green)		2.00	5.00	15.00	30.00	60.00					
Plate 30, bottom	Slag or Onyx (other colors)		3.00	7.00	20.00	40.00	75.00					
Plate 30, upper right	Brick		25.00	30.00	45.00	85.00						
Plate 30, upper left	Oxblood (clear or white)		8.00	15.00	20.00	35.00						
Plate 30, top	Oxblood (egg yolk, lemonade, cobalt, or green)		75.00	85.00	100.00	125.00						
Plate 30, lower right	Cork screws (1 color, white base)		1.00	3.50	10.00							
Plate 30, lower right and Plate 31, lower right (box)	Corkscrews (1 color, non-white base)		3.00	5.00	20.00							
Plate 30, lower right and Plate 31, lower right (box)	Corkscrew (tri-color)		7.50	10.00	30.00							
Plate 30, lower left	Popeye (yellow with red, blue, or green)		7.50	12.00								
Plate 30, lower left	Popeye (other colors)		15.00	25.00								

157

SULPHIDES

Domestic Animals, Birds, and Pets
(Examples in Figs. 6-5, 6-6, and 6-9)

Camel	$ 180		Hen	
Cat			pecking ground	225
on haunches	100		setting	150
lying down	150		Horse	
Cow			running	180
grazing	100		other positions	130
other position	150		saddled	300
Dog	150		Parrot	200
sitting or on haunches	75		Pig	200
lying down	150		Ram	250
sitting and begging	250		Rooster	100
bird in mouth	600		Sheep or lamb	
Donkey	250		standing	75
Duck	180		lying down	130
wings spread	500			
Goat				
head forward	100			
biting back	250			

Wild Animals and Birds
(Examples in Figs. 6-2, 6-3, 6-7, and 6-8)

Bird			Lion	
short tail	$ 100		standing	100
long tail	100		sitting or lying down	200
Bear			Lizard on rock	350
standing all 4's	75		Lobster	1,750
standing hindlegs	100		Love birds (facing pair)	1,000
sitting on haunches	180		Mouse (rat)	350
Buffalo	250		Otter (mink, weasel, etc.)	225
Crane (freestanding)	300		Owl	
Deer	250		wings down	170
Eagle	120		wings spread	350
Elephant	100		Rabbit	
Fish	130		running or on haunches	100
Fox	180		sitting up, hind legs	180
Frog	200		Squirrel	100
Hedgehog	100		Swan, open neck	500
Heron catching fish			Vulture	450
(in relief on tablet)	300			

People, Monkeys, and Miscellaneous
(Examples in Figs. 6-4, 6-10, and 6-11)

Adults		child bathing		500
cellist	$1,750	in chair		500
clown, peaked cap	750	kneeling and praying		750
hunter/deer, (relief on tablet)	1,750	girl		
man		sitting with doll		500
holding hat	1,000	with croquet mallet and ball		750
on stump	750	papoose on cradle board		1,000
(with musket) and woman	4,000	two children		
prospector	1,750	(or mother/daughter) reading		2,000
santa/old man	2,000	Busts		
two dancers	4,000	Beethoven, Columbus,		
woman in long dress	750	Jenny Lind, President Garfield,		
Children		etc.		2,000+
baby	500	Monkeys, Chimps, Miscellaneous		
in basket	500	ape man		300
boy		clothed creature with instrument		600
on knees with sailboat	500	monkey		
on stump	500	standing on all fours		200
with horn on hobby horse	500	seated		350
		seated wearing hat		500

Religious, Objects, Insects, and Numbers
(Examples in Figs. 6-12 and 6-13)

Religious		Insects	
angel		honeybee	1,800
with wreath	$ 750	Numbers	
in tunic (praying)	900	1-9, freestanding	450
head and wings	2,000	on coin or disk	700
Christ on the cross	750	0 or double digit	1,000
Objects			
Indian head penny	1,500		
pocket watch	1,250		

Colored Glass, Figures, and Double Figures
(Examples on Plates 26, 27, 28B and Fig. 6-2)

Figures in colored glass	$2,500+	Colored numbers	3,500+
Colored animals (2 colors)	3,500+	Two separate figures	5,000+

CARPET BOWLS*
(Examples on Plates 6 and 7)

Lined	$ 90	Sponge and spatter	250
Dot and crown	110	Flowers, shamrocks, and tan base	350
Other "spot" and banded cross	160	Jack	45
Bullseye	200	with logo	175

*(See Chapter 3, Carpet Bowls for news on reproductions.)

PELTIER COMICS
(Examples on Plate 31, center box)

		Kayo	250
Andy	$110	Koko	75
Annie	85	Moon	110
Betty	110	Sandy	100
Bimbo	40	Skeezix	85
Emma	40	Smitty	40
Herbie	40		

Credits

OWNERSHIP OF MARBLES IN PLATES

The following list credits collectors whose marbles were photographed for the plates in this book. Marbles and collectors are listed by plate, but individual marbles are not identified by position within a plate. My apologies to Bucky Zelesky who was particularly patient in awaiting the return of his marbles; I have decided to list contributors within each plate alphabetically. Over 1,000 of the marbles and carpet bowls pictured in this book are from the author's personal collection.

Plate 1. Stone, Agate, and Semiprecious Stones.
  Jamie Browder: large green agate, blue agates (2), opal.
Plate 2. Clay and Benningtons.
  Dave Johnson: painted clays.
Plate 3. Crockery and Stoneware.
  Jamie Browder: stoneware with turquoise.
Plate 4. China Lines, Leaves, and Bullseyes.
  Sue Cooper: black double bullseye with leaves; mid-sized doughnut bullseye; broad-banded red, green, and blue; broad-banded, red, green, and black.
  Dick Davidson: large doughnut bullseye.
  Tom Ecker: red double coil and green leaves; black double coil and red leaves; solid bullseyes (2); small doughnut bullseyes (2); 3 single lines, red, black, and blue; broad red band and 3 blue lines; 1 wide blue, 5 red, and 5 green lines.
  Brian Estepp: red double bullseye with leaves.
Plate 5. China Flowers and Geometrics.
  Beverly Brule: segmented with different colors, red doughnut/geometric, red and green geometric, green band and blue dot stencil, coil with red and green geometric, open rose, blue helix and flower.
  Sue Cooper: red segmented with leaves, red hemispherical lines and shamrock.
  Tom Ecker: blue helix and straight flower; red geometric, red hemispherical lines, and green geometric; helix with a red and green geometric; intersecting helixes with leaves; coil with red geometric.

Elizabeth Reeb: red dot stencil wreath, red hemispherical lines and green geometric.

Plate 6. Carpet Bowls and Jacks.
Lorain Altshuler: 2 tan base bowls.
Beverly Brule: small blue bullseye.
Sue Cooper: blue shamrock.
Roger Matile: black dot and doughnut, jack with logo (Jaques).

Plate 7. Carpet Bowls.
Roger Matile: green and black lined.

Plate 8. Latticinio Cores (White or Yellow).
Author's collection.

Plate 9. Unusual Latticinio Cores.
Author's collection.

Plate 10. Ridged and Column Solid Cores.
Author's collection.

Plate 11. Unusual Solid Cores (Colored Base).
Author's collection.

Plate 12. Divided Cores (3 & 4 Strand).
Author's collection.

Plate 13. Ribbon and Unusual Divided Cores.
Jamie Browder: thick single ribbon.
Bucky Zelesky: blue multilevel divided core.

Plate 14. Onionskin and Ribbon Lutz.
Jamie Browder: multicolored onionskin Lutz (2), yellow onionskin Lutz.
Earl Hogue: "Spheroidals" box containing green and yellow onionskin Lutz.

Plate 15. Banded Lutz: Clear, Colored and Opaque.
Jamie Browder: green translucent Lutz, white opaque Lutz with green stripes.
Bucky Zelesky: large ($2\frac{1}{8}''$) blue-banded clear Lutz.

Plate 16. Colored Glass with Outer Decoration.
Jamie Browder: 3 colored glass with outer bands—1) red, 2) blue, and 3) amber; green submarine.

Plate 17. Colored Glass with Inner Decoration.
Jamie Browder: green glass marble, purple glass marble.

Plates 18A and B. Mist/Peppermint and Undecorated Opaques.
Jamie Browder: peppermint with mica.
Bucky Zelesky: large ($1\frac{5}{8}''$) peppermint.

Plate 19. Clambroths.
Scott Strasburger: large ($2''$) clam with blue lines, large ($1\frac{3}{4}''$) clam with red lines, large ($1\frac{3}{8}''$) clam with blue lines, large ($1\frac{3}{8}''$) clam with green lines, clam with green and blue lines.
Bucky Zelesky: largest ($2\frac{1}{8}''$) black clam, black clam with red lines (2), black clam with blue lines, black clam with yellow lines, black clam with yellow and white lines.

Plate 20. Banded Opaques and Indians.

Jamie Browder: red-banded Indian; pink pastel with yellow and brown bands; green pastel with orange and red bands; yellow pastel with dark red bands; chartreuse pastel with red bands and brown and red bands; blue pastel with red, white, and yellow bands.

Plate 21. Mica Marbles.
Bucky Zelesky: red micas (2).

Plate 22. Segmented Onionskins.
Author's collection.

Plate 23. Non-segmented Onionskins.
Jamie Browder: 4 lobed, red and turquoise onionskins.
Bucky Zelesky: blue onionskin with mica panels, red and yellow onionskin with mica panels.

Plate 24. A Variety of Small Swirls.
Jamie Browder: solid core, yellow; solid core, blue; solid core, green; peppermint with mica.

Plate 25. End-of-Day, Cloud, and Paperweight.
Jamie Browder: End-of-Day with mica.

Plate 26. Sulphides in Colored Glass.
Earl Hogue: elephant in blue, lion in green, bear in yellow.

Plate 27. Colored Figure Sulphides.
Anonymous: blue no. 1, green no. 8.
Bucky Zelesky: woman, dark hair and blue neckline.

Plate 28A. Roman Glass Marbles.
Larry Prince.

Plate 28B. Tri-Color Horse Sulphide.
Art Ward.

Plate 28C. Mark Matthews Marbles.
Author's Collection.

Plate 28D. Latticinio Ribbons and Banded Latticinio.
Author's Collection.

Plate 28E. Orange/White and Orange/Yellow Latticinio.
Author's Collection.

Plate 29. Transition Marbles.
Brian Estepp: large (1¼″) purple and white Navarre type, brown and white Navarre type, purple and white Navarre type, medium-green and white Navarre type.

Plate 30. Machine-Made Marbles.
Jamie Browder: Tom Mix comic, Cotes Master Loaf comic.
Brian Estepp: entire plate except for Peltier comics.

Plate 31. Machine-Made in Original Boxes.
Gary Dolly: entire plate of boxes except guineas and Peltier cerise agates.
Brian Estepp: Christensen Agate Co. (Cambridge) Guineas.

Plate 32. Marble Games.
Jamie Browder: Panama Pile Driver with cart.
Dave Johnson: Panama Pile Driver, early version.

OWNERSHIP OF MARBLES IN FIGURES.

Fig. 6-1. Sulphides, Original Box of Twelve.
    Frank Gardenhire.
Fig. 6-2. Sulphides, Fish, Amphibians, and Reptiles.
    Author's collection.
Fig. 6-3. Sulphides, Wild Birds.
    Roland Baker: vulture.
    Jamie Browder: large eagle.
    Brian Estepp: heron eating fish.
Fig. 6-4. Sulphides, Adults.
    Anonymous: bust of Beethoven.
    Lloyd Huffer: man with musket and woman standing.
Fig. 6-5. Sulphides, Dogs and Cats.
    Author's collection.
Fig. 6-6. Sulphides, Domestic Animals.
    Author's collection.
Fig. 6-7. Sulphides, Small Wild Animals.
    Dave Johnson: weasel or ermine.
Fig. 6-8. Sulphides, Large Wild Animals.
    Author's collection.
Fig. 6-9. Sulphides, Domestic Birds.
    Author's collection.
Fig. 6-10. Sulphides, Monkeys.
    Brian Estepp: mythological figure with drum.
Fig. 6-11. Sulphides, Children.
    Roland Baker: girl with croquet mallet and ball.
Fig. 6-12. Sulphides, Religious.
    Author's collection.
Fig. 6-13. Sulphides, Numbers.
    Author's collection.

References

Bachman, M. 1985. Der Universal Spielwaren Katalog, German Toys 1924–1926. Hobby House Press, Inc.: Cumberland, MD.

Barlow, R.E. and J.E. Kaiser. 1987. *A Guide to Sandwich Glass, Witch Balls, Containers and Toys.* Barlow-Kaiser Publishing Co.: Ind. Windham, NH.

Biernacki, C. March 1984. "Carpet Balls," *City & Country Home Collecting*, pp. 64–66.

Beuschel, R.M. 1988. *Pinball 1—Illustrated Historical Guide to Pinball Machines, vol. 1.* Hoflin Publishing Ltd.: Wheat Ridge, CO.

Carskadden, J. and R. Gartley. 1990(A). "A Preliminary Seriation of 19th-Century Decorated Porcelain Marbles," *Historical Archaeology*, 24:55–69.

Carskadden, J. and R. Gartley. 1990(B). *Chinas—Hand-Painted Marbles of the Late 19th Century.* McClain Printing Company: Parsons, WV.

Carskadden, J., R. Gartley, and E. Reeb. 1985. "Marble Making and Marble Playing in Eastern Ohio: The Significance of Ceramic, Stone, and Glass Marbles in Historic Archaeology," Proceedings of the Symposium on Ohio Valley Urban and Historic Archaeology. Donald B. Ball and Philip J. DiBlasi, ed. Ohio Historical Society. Columbus, OH., pp. 86–97.

Carskadden, J. and M. Randall. 1987. "The Christensen Agate Company, Cambridge, Ohio, 1927–1933," *Muskingum Annals, Number Four.* Published by The Muskingum Valley Archaeological Survey: Zanesville, OH., pp. 48–52.

Charleston, R.J. 1984. "English Glass and the Glass Used in England, *circa* 400–1940," *English Decorative Arts.* Series Editor: Hugh Wakefield.

Cohill, M. *M.F. Christensen and The Perfect Glass Ball Machine.* America's First Machine-Made Glass Toy Marble Factory. Vol. 1, Series 1. The History of the American Toy Marble Industry. Group Ideate Publishing: Akron, OH.

Collectors Roundup. Jan. 24, 1947. "Marbles Have History, Too."

Everhart, J.F. 1882. *History of Muskingum County, Ohio.* A.A. Graham: Columbus, OH.

Ferretti, F. 1973. *The Great American Marble Book.* Workman Publishing Co.: New York, NY.

Ferretti, F. 1974. "The Great American Marble Game," *Pastimes: Inflight Entertainment for the Passengers of Eastern Airlines.* Pastimes Publications, Inc.: NY., pp. 12–17.

Fisher, C.C. 1975. *Navarre, A Little Town and Its People.* Navarre Bethlehem Township Historical Society.

Gartley, R. and J. Carskadden. 1987. Marbles from an Irish Channel Cistern, New Orleans, Louisiana. Proceedings of the Symposium on Ohio Valley Urban and Historic Archaeology, vol. V. Donald B. Ball and Philip J. DiBlasi, ed. Wickliffe Mounds Research Center, Wickliffe, KY., pp. 112–125.

Gates, B. 1968. "It's spring—get out your aggies & immies," *Changing Times, The Kiplinger Magazine,* pp. 46–47.

Grist, E. *Antique & Collectible Marbles: Identification & Values.* Collectors Books, Schroeder Publishing Co., Inc.: Paducah, KY.

Grist, E. and G. Grist. 1983. *Marbles at Auction.* Privately printed: Ft. Scott, KS.

Lee, R.W. 1966. *Sandwich Glass.* Lee Publications: Wellesley Hills, MA.

Menke, F.G. 1953. *The Encyclopaedia of Sports.* Cited in: Biernacki, C., 1984. Carpet Balls.

Mentor, The. April 1927. "Prehistoric Boys Played Marbles Too," p. 63.

Miller, R.C. 1966. "Swirl and Sulphide Playing Marbles," *The Spinning Wheel,* November, pp. 20–21.

Morrison, M. and C. Terison. *Marbles: Identification and Price Guide.* Privately published, Falmouth, ME.

Navarre—The Evening Independant, Massillon, Ohio. A. 1950s? Ohio's First White Settlement Was Founded in Navarre. B. April 18, 1961 (Title Unknown).

Patten, G.E. 1869. "Marbles," *Appleton's Journal, A Weekly Paper,* no. 20, Saturday, August 14 issue.

Randall, M.E. 1971. "Early Marbles," *Historical Archaeology.* David A. Armour, ed. The Society for Historical Archaeology: Lansing, MI., pp. 102–105.

Ibid. 1979. *Marbles as Historical Artifacts.* Marbles Collectors Society of America: Trumbull, CT.

Randall, M.E. and D. Webb. 1988. *Greenberg's Guide to Marbles.* Marsha A. Davis, ed. Greenberg Publishing Co., Inc.: Sykesville, MD.

Revi, A.C. 1959. *Nineteenth Century Glass.* Thomas Nelson and Sons: New York, NY.

Roberts, A.W. 1883. "Marbles and Where They Come From," *Harpers Young People.*

Runyan, C.C. 1985. *Knuckles Down! A Fun Guide to Marble Play.* Right Brain Publishing: Kansas City, MO.

Shetrone, C. and E.F. Greenman. 1931. "Explorations of the Seip Group of Prehistoric Earthworks," *Ohio Archaeological and Historical Quarterly,* pp. 349–509.

Schneider, N.F. 1957. Clay Industry. Zanesville *Times Signal.*

Stout, W. 1923. Coal Formation Clays of Ohio. *Bulletin* No. 26 (4th Series), Geological Survey of Ohio, Columbus.

Marble Collectors Clubs

Marble Collector's Society of America
P.O. Box 222
Trumbull, CT 06611

Marbles Collectors Unlimited
P.O. Box 206
Northboro, MA 01532

National Marble Club of America
440 Eaton Road
Drexel Hill, PA 19026

Index